ExpressWays

ENGLISH FOR COMMUNICATION

3A

Steven J. Molinsky · Bill Bliss

Prentice Hall Regents, Englewood Cliffs, NJ 07632

Library of Congress Cataloging in Publication Data

Molinsky, Steven J.
  ExpressWays: English for communication.

  Includes index.
    1. English language—Text-books for foreign speakers.
I. Bliss, Bill. II. Title.
PE1128.M674 1986   428.3'4   85-30059
ISBN 0-13-298274-9 (set)
ISBN 0-13-298282-X (3A)
ISBN 0-13-298316-8 (3B)

Editorial/production supervision and interior design: Sylvia Moore
Development: Ellen Lehrburger
Notes and Commentary section: Carla Meskill
Cover design: Lundgren Graphics Ltd.
Manufacturing buyer: Harry P. Baisley
Page layout: Diane Koromhas

Illustrations and Cover Drawing by Gabriel Polonsky

Printed in the United States of America

10 9 8 7 6

ISBN 0-13-298282-X

Prentice-Hall International, Inc., *London*
Prentice-Hall of Australia Pty. Limited, *Sydney*
Editora Prentice-Hall do Brasil, Ltda., *Rio de Janeiro*
Prentice-Hall Canada Inc., *Toronto*
Prentice-Hall Hispanoamericana, S.A., *Mexico*
Prentice-Hall of India Private Limited, *New Delhi*
Prentice-Hall of Japan, Inc., *Tokyo*
Prentice-Hall of Southeast Asia Pte. Ltd., *Singapore*
Whitehall Books Limited, *Wellington, New Zealand*

Contents

GRAMMAR: Adjectives • Declarative Sentences with Question Intonation • Embedded Questions • Indirect Objects • One/Ones • Passives • Past Continuous Tense • Past Tense • Sequence of Tenses • Superlatives • Tag Questions

FUNCTIONS: Instructing • Directions-Location • Asking for and Reporting Information • Requests
CONVERSATION STRATEGIES: Asking for Repetition • Checking and Indicating Understanding

GRAMMAR: Embedded Questions • Gerunds • Imperatives • Partitives • Question Formation • Sequence of Tenses

FUNCTIONS: Satisfaction/Dissatisfaction • Likes/Dislikes • Complimenting • Disappointment • Complaining • Advice-Suggestions

GRAMMAR: Adjectives • Comparatives • Gerunds • Infinitives • Negative Questions • Present Continuous Tense to Express Habitual Action • Singular/Plural • Superlatives • Too/Enough • Would

FUNCTIONS: Preference • Want-Desire • Indifference
CONVERSATION STRATEGY: Hesitating

GRAMMAR: Gerunds • Infinitives • Partitives • Present Perfect Tense • Sequence of Tenses • Want + Object + Infinitive • Whether • WH-ever Words • Would

TO THE TEACHER

ExpressWays is a functional English program for adult and young-adult learners of English. The program consists of the following components:

Student Course Books—offering intensive conversational practice;
Companion Workbooks—offering grammar, reading, writing, and listening comprehension practice fully coordinated with the student course books;
Guide Books—providing background notes and expansion activities for all lessons and step-by-step instructions for teachers;
Audio Program—offering realistic presentation of dialogs in the texts;
Placement and Achievement Testing Program—providing tools for the evaluation of student levels and progress.

ExpressWays—Book 3 is intended for students who have been exposed to the essentials of intermediate-level grammar and who have already mastered the usage of English for everyday life situations. The text builds upon and reinforces this foundation and prepares students for higher level language skills required for effective interpersonal communication. *ExpressWays—Book 3* is organized functionally, while incorporating integrated coverage of grammar and topics.

THE DIMENSIONS OF COMMUNICATION: FUNCTION, FORM, AND CONTENT

A number of texts present the functional syllabus by describing language use and listing sets of functional phrases. The exercises and activities that normally accompany these descriptions and lists usually occur in isolation, rather than being totally integrated into active conversational practice. In addition, traditional functional approaches usually do not give students intensive communicative practice using the correct grammatical forms that are required by particular functional language choices.

ExpressWays, essentially, does not seek to provide students with background knowledge about language use. Rather, it provides dynamic, communicative practice that involves students in lively interactions based on the content of real-life contexts and situations. The functional syllabus is fully integrated into a complete conversational course in which students not only learn the various ways to express each function, but also intensively practice the grammatical forms required to turn functional expressions into lines of effective communication in English.

Every lesson in the program offers students simultaneous practice with one or more functions, the grammatical forms needed to express those functions competently, and the contexts and situations in which the functions and grammar are used. This "tri-dimensional clustering" of function, form, and content is the organizing principle behind each lesson and the cornerstone of the *ExpressWays* approach to functionai syllabus design.

ExpressWays aims to offer students broad exposure to uses of language in a variety of relevant contexts: in community, academic, employment, home, and social settings.

The characters portrayed are people of different ages, ethnic groups, and occupations, interacting in real-life situations.

While some texts make a point of giving students a range of ways of expressing a function, from extremely polite to very impolite, we have chosen to "take the middle ground" and concentrate on those expressions that would most frequently occur in normal polite conversation between people in various settings. *ExpressWays* does offer a variety of registers, from the formal language someone might use in a job interview, with a customer, or when speaking with an authority figure, to the informal language someone would use when talking with family members, co-workers, or friends. When appropriate, the text also presents students with alternative degrees of expressing a function, such as strength of disagreement and certainty or the directness of requests and advice.

A special feature of the program is the treatment of discourse strategies. Students actively practice initiating conversations and topics, interrupting, hesitating, asking for clarification, and other conversation skills.

AN OVERVIEW

Guided Conversations

Guided Conversations are the dialogs and exercises that are the central learning devices in the program. Each lesson begins with a model guided conversation that illustrates the use of one or more functions and the structures they require, all in the context of a meaningful exchange of communication. Key functional expressions in the models are in bold-face type and are footnoted, referring students to short lists of alternative expressions for accomplishing the functions. In the exercises that follow, students create new conversations by placing new contexts, content, or characters into the framework of the model, and by using any of the alternative functional expressions.

"Now Present Your Own Conversations"

Each lesson ends with this open-ended exercise which offers students the opportunity to create and present original conversations based on the model and any of the alternative expressions. Students contribute content based on their experiences, ideas, and imaginations, while staying within the framework of the model.

We should emphasize that the objective of each lesson is to provide a measure of controlled practice with a dialog and guided conversation exercises so that students can competently use functional expressions in creating their own original conversations.

Interchange

This end-of-chapter activity offers students the opportunity to create and to present "guided role plays." Each activity consists of a model that students can practice and then use as a basis for their original presentations. Students should be encouraged to be inventive and to use new vocabulary in these presentations and should feel free to adapt and expand the model any way they wish.

Scenes & Improvisations

These "free role plays" appear after every third chapter, offering review and synthesis of functions and conversation strategies in the three preceding chapters. Students are presented with eight scenes depicting conversations between people in various situations. They use the information in the scenes to determine who the people are and what they are talking about. Then, students improvise based on their perceptions of the scenes' characters, contexts, and situations.

The purpose of these improvisations is to offer recombination practice that promotes students' absorption of the preceding chapters' functions and strategies into their repertoire of active language use.

Support and Reference Sections

ExpressWays offers a number of support and reference sections:

- *Chapter Opening Pages* provide an overview of functions and conversation strategies highlighted in each chapter.
- *End-of-Chapter Summaries* provide complete lists of expressions for the functions and conversation strategies appearing in each chapter.
- An *Inventory of Functions and Conversation Strategies* in the Appendix offers a comprehensive display of all expressions for the functions and conversation strategies in the text, and indicates the chapters in which the expressions appear.
- A *Notes and Commentary* section in the Appendix provides background information for each lesson, including notes on language usage, grammar, and culture; commentaries on the characters, contexts, and situations; and explanations of idiomatic and colloquial expressions.
- An *Index of Functions and Conversation Strategies* and an *Index of Grammatical Structures* provide a convenient reference for locating coverage of functions and grammar in the text.

THE TOTAL *ExpressWays* PROGRAM

The *ExpressWays Student Course Books* are essentially designed to offer intensive communicative practice with functional language. These texts may be used independently or in conjunction with the *ExpressWays Companion Workbooks,* which offer practice in the other skill areas of reading, writing, and listening, as well as focused practice with particular grammar structures as they occur in the program. Each exercise in the Companion Workbook indicates the specific Student Course Book page that it corresponds to.

The *ExpressWays Guide Books* provide step-by-step instructions for coverage of each lesson, background notes, sample answers to guided conversation exercises, and answer keys and listening-activity scripts for exercises in the Companion Workbooks. Perhaps the most important feature of the Guide Books is the expansion exercise that is recommended for each lesson. These exercises offer students free, spontaneous practice with the functional content that is treated in a more systematic manner in the text itself. Activities include improvisations, "information gap" role plays, problem-solving, and topics for discussion and debate. We encourage teachers to use these activities or similar ones as springboards to help their students "break away" from the text and incorporate lesson content into their everyday use of English.

The *ExpressWays Audio Program* includes a set of tapes providing realistic presentation of all model dialogs and selected guided conversation exercises in the Student Course Books. The tapes are designed to be used interactively, so that the recorded voice serves as the student's speaking partner, making conversation practice possible even when the student is studying alone. The Audio Program also includes a set of tapes for the listening comprehension exercises in the Companion Workbooks.

The *ExpressWays Testing Program* includes a Placement Testing Kit for initial evaluation and leveling of students, and sets of Mid-Term and Final Examinations to measure students' achievement at each level of the program. All tests in the program include both oral and written evaluation components.

SUGGESTED TEACHING STRATEGIES

In using *ExpressWays*, we encourage you to develop approaches and strategies that are compatible with your own teaching style and the needs and abilities of your students. While the program does not require any specific method or technique in order to be used effectively, you may find it helpful to review and try out some of the following suggestions. (Specific step-by-step instructions may be found in the Guide Books.)

Guided Conversations

1. *Listening.* With books closed, have students listen to the model conversation—presented by you, a pair of students, or on the audio tape.
2. *Discussion.* Have students discuss the model conversation: Who are the people? What is the situation?

   (At this point, you may want to call students' attention to any related language or culture notes, which can be found in the Appendix to the Student Course Book and in the Guide Book.)
3. *Reading.* With books open, have students follow along as two students present the model.
4. *Practice.* In pairs, small groups, or as a class, have students practice the model conversation.
5. *Alternative Expressions.* Present to the class each sentence of the dialog containing a footnoted expression. Call on different students to present the same sentence, but replacing the footnoted expression with its alternatives. (You can cue students to do this quickly by asking, "What's another way of saying that?" or "How else could he/she/you say that?")
6. *Pair Practice.* (optional) Have pairs of students simultaneously practice all the exercises, using the footnoted expressions or any of their alternatives.
7. *Presentation.* Call on pairs of students to present the exercises, using the footnoted expressions or any of their alternatives. Before students present, "set the scene" by describing the characters and the context or have the students do this themselves.

   (Discuss any language or culture notes related to the exercises, as indicated in the Student Course Book Appendix and the Guide Book.)

"Now Present Your Own Conversations"

In these activities that follow the guided conversations at the end of each lesson, have pairs of students create and present original conversations based on the model and any of the alternative expressions. Encourage students to be inventive as they create their characters and situations. (You may want to assign this exercise as homework, having students prepare their original conversations, practice them the next day with another student, and then present them to the class. In this way, students can review the previous day's lesson without actually having to repeat the specific exercises already covered.)

Expansion

We encourage you to use the expansion activity for each lesson suggested in the Guide Book or a similar activity that provides students with free, spontaneous practice while synthesizing the content of the lesson.

Interchange

Have students practice the model using the same steps listed above for guided conversations. Then have pairs of students create and present original conversations using the model dialog as a guide. Encourage students to be inventive and to use new vocabulary. (You may want to assign this exercise as homework, having students prepare their conversations, practice them the next day with another student, and then present them to the class.) Students should present their conversations without referring to the written text, but they should also not memorize them. Rather, they should feel free to adapt and expand them any way they wish.

Scenes & Improvisations

Have students talk about the people and the situations, and then present role plays based on the scenes. Students may refer back to previous lessons as a resource, but they should not simply re-use specific conversations. (You may want to assign these exercises as written homework, having students prepare their conversations, practice them the next day with another student, and then present them to the class.)

Review

You will notice that most functions and conversation strategies occur at several different points in the text. We have built a system of spiraling into the design of the program, so that content is reviewed and expanded upon at regular intervals. We encourage you to provide continual review practice based on your students' needs. Students may find it especially helpful to have frequent focused reviews of many of the alternative expressions for specific functions and conversation strategies. One useful technique is to have a pair of students present a model conversation from a previous lesson while other students listen with books closed. Stop the presentation after any line that contains a footnoted expression and ask different students to present the same line, but replacing the footnoted expression with its alternatives. (You can cue students to do this quickly by asking, "What's another way of saying that?" or "How else could he/she/you say that?")

In conclusion, we have attempted to offer students a communicative, meaningful, and lively way of practicing the functions of English, along with the grammar structures needed to express them competently. While conveying to you the substance of our textbook, we hope that we have also conveyed the spirit: that learning to communicate in English can be genuinely interactive . . . truly relevant to our students' lives . . . and fun!

Steven J. Molinsky
Bill Bliss

A NOTE ABOUT USING THE FOOTNOTES

Here are the conventions that you will need to know in order to use the footnotes containing alternative expressions in each lesson.

1. In the model conversation, a bold-faced footnoted expression indicates that there are alternative ways of expressing this function. Sometimes this expression is an entire sentence, and sometimes it is only a portion of a sentence.

2. ( ) indicates that the word or words are optional. For example, the footnote:

    I'm (very) sorry to hear (about) that. = I'm sorry to hear that.
    I'm very sorry to hear that.
    I'm sorry to hear about that.
    I'm very sorry to hear about that.

3. / indicates that the words on either side of the / mark are interchangeable. For example, the footnote:

    I don't/can't believe it! = I don't believe it!
    I can't believe it!

4. Sometimes the ( ) and / symbols appear together. For example, the footnote:

    I'm not (completely/absolutely) positive. = I'm not positive.
    I'm not completely positive.
    I'm not absolutely positive.

5. Sometimes the footnote indicates that an alternative expression requires a change in the grammar of the sentence. For example, the footnote:

    How about _____ing?   How about going shopping?
    Let's _____.   =   Let's go shopping.
    What if we _____ed?   What if we went shopping?

Components of an ExpressWays Lesson

A **model conversation** offers initial practice with the functions and structures of the lesson.

Key functional expressions are in bold-face type and are footnoted, referring students to a box containing alternative expressions for accomplishing the functions.

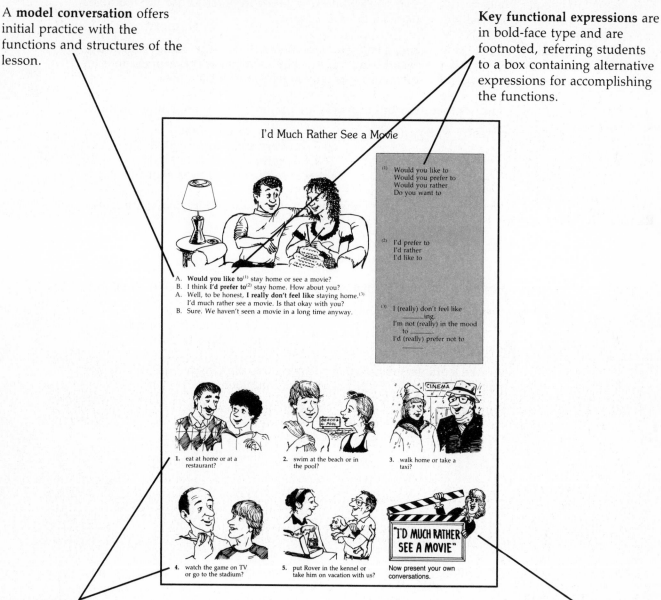

I'd Much Rather See a Movie

(1) Would you like to
Would you prefer to
Would you rather
Do you want to

(2) I'd prefer to
I'd rather
I'd like to

(3) I (really) don't feel like
___ing.
I'm not (really) in the mood to ___.
I'd (really) prefer not to ___.

A. **Would you like to**[1] stay home or see a movie?
B. I think **I'd prefer to**[2] stay home. How about you?
A. Well, to be honest, **I really don't feel like** staying home.[3] I'd much rather see a movie. Is that okay with you?
B. Sure. We haven't seen a movie in a long time anyway.

1. eat at home or at a restaurant?
2. swim at the beach or in the pool?
3. walk home or take a taxi?
4. watch the game on TV or go to the stadium?
5. put Rover in the kennel or take him on vacation with us?

"I'D MUCH RATHER SEE A MOVIE"

Now present your own conversations.

In the **exercises,** students create conversations by placing new contexts, content, or characters into the model, and by using any of the alternative functional expressions.

The **open-ended exercise** at the end of each lesson asks students to create and present original conversations based on the model and any of the alternative expressions.

For example:

Exercise 1 might be completed by placing the new exercise content into the existing model:

A. Would you like to eat at home or at a restaurant?
B. I think I'd prefer to eat at home. How about you?
A. Well, to be honest, I really don't feel like eating at home. I'd much rather eat at a restaurant. Is that okay with you?
B. Sure. We haven't eaten at a restaurant in a long time anyway.

Exercise 2 might be completed by using the new exercise content *and* some of the alternative functional expressions:

A. Would you prefer to swim at the beach or in the pool?
B. I think I'd like to swim at the beach. How about you?
A. Well, to be honest, I'm not really in the mood to swim at the beach. I'd much rather swim in the pool. Is that okay with you?
B. Sure. We haven't swum in the pool in a long time anyway.

I Don't Think We've Met
Let Me Introduce . . .
Don't I Know You from Somewhere?
Guess Who I Saw Yesterday!

• Negative Questions • One/Ones • Relative Clauses
with Who/Whose • Used to/Would • WH-Questions

I Don't Think We've Met

Carmen Kenji

(1) My name is
I'm

(2) Hello.

[less formal]
Hi.

[more formal]
How do you do?

(3) (It's) nice to meet you.
(It's) nice meeting you.
(I'm) happy to meet you.
(I'm) glad to meet you.
(I'm) pleased to meet you.

(4) How about you?
What about you?
And you?

Where are you from?

A. I don't think we've met. **My name is**(1) Carmen.
B. **Hello.**(2) **I'm**(1) Kenji. **Nice to meet you.**(3)
A. **Nice meeting you,**(3) too. Where are you from?
B. Japan. **How about you?**(4)
A. Venezuela.

Tom Carol

What do you do?

1. dancer
English teacher

Arlene Betty

Which apartment do you live in?

2. 2C
4D

Pedro Nick

How long have you been studying here?

3. two months
one year

Ted Carl

Who is your doctor?

ANN MURPHY M.D.
PETER GOLD M.D.

4. Dr. Murphy
Dr. Gold

Frank — Gloria

5. Accounting
Shipping

Lois — Bob

6. History
Chemistry

Jane — Sally

7. the morning shift
the night shift

Alan — Ruth

8. the bride's
the groom's

Steve — Judy

9. a lawyer
a journalist

Paul — Dave

10. rock
jazz

Donna — Martha

11. next month
any day now

Now present your own conversations.

Let Me Introduce . . .

(1) How are you?
How have you been?

[less formal]
How are you doing?
How are things?
How's it going?

(2) Fine (thank you/thanks).
Good.
All right.
Okay.
Not bad.

(3) Let me introduce (you to)
I'd like to introduce (you to)
I'd like you to meet

[less formal]
Meet
This is

A. Hi! **How are you?**(1)
B. **Fine.**(2) And you?
A. **Fine, thanks.**(2) **Let me introduce you to**(3) my friend Paul.
B. Nice to meet you.

1. my brother Tom

2. my sister Kate

3. my roommate, Peter

4. my English teacher, Mrs. Simon

5. my fiancé, Steve Smith

Now present your own conversations.

Don't I Know You from Somewhere?

I know her from somewhere. She works at the bank on Main Street.

BUS STOP

A. **Excuse me,**[1] but don't I know you from somewhere?
B. No, I don't think so.
A. **Sure.**[2] Don't you work at the bank on Main Street?
B. No, I'm afraid not. You must have me **confused**[3] with somebody else.
A. Oh, **I'm sorry.**[4] I guess I made a mistake.

[1] Excuse me.
Pardon me.

[2] Sure.
Of course.

[3] confused
mixed up

[4] I'm sorry.
Excuse me.

We've met before. He just moved into the new house up the street.

1.

I know him from somewhere. His daughter is on the same baseball team as my son.

2.

We've met somewhere. We were classmates at Longfellow High School.

3.

I've seen her on TV. She's a news reporter for Channel 5.

4.

I've seen his face somewhere. He's on the FBI's "10 Most Wanted" list!*

5.

"DON'T I KNOW YOU FROM SOMEWHERE?"

Now present your own conversations.

*Federal Bureau of Investigation

5

Guess Who I Saw Yesterday!

Kathy Wilson
She saved my life when
I almost drowned at
the beach last year.

A. **Guess**[1] who I **saw**[2] yesterday!
B. Who?
A. Kathy Wilson!
B. Kathy Wilson? I don't think I remember her.
A. Oh, sure you do! She's the one who saved my life when I almost drowned at the beach last year.
B. Oh, of course. Now I remember her. How IS she?
A. **Pretty good.**[3]
B. Did she have anything to say?
A. Not really. We just talked **for a minute.**[4] But it was really good to see her again.

The Bradley twins
Their parents used to dress
them alike all the time.

A. **You won't believe**[1] who I **ran into**[2] yesterday!
B. Who?
A. The Bradley twins!
B. The Bradley twins? I don't think I remember them.
A. Oh, sure you do. They're the ones whose parents used to dress them alike all the time.
B. Oh, of course. Now I remember them. How ARE they?
A. **Fine.**[3]
B. Did they have anything to say?
A. Not really. We just talked **for a moment.**[4] But it was really good to see them again.

[1] Guess	[2] saw	[3] Pretty good.	[4] for a minute
You won't believe	ran into	Fine.	for a moment
	bumped into	She looks terrific/	for a few minutes
		great/fine.	for a few seconds

1. Professor Kingston
He taught Economic Theory at Business School.

2. Mr. and Mrs. Larson
They used to live next door to us when we lived across town.

3. Miss Hubbard
Her car would always break down in front of our house.

4. The Bennetts
Their daughter baby-sits for us every once in a while.

5. Lucy Crawford
She's the head of the Board of Education.

6. Patty Taylor
She had a crush on me in the sixth grade.

7. Mr. and Mrs. Miller
They're retired and living in Florida now.

8. Eddie Long
He was my high school sweetheart.

9. Butch Baker
His dog would always get loose and scare all the children in the neighborhood.

"GUESS WHO I SAW YESTERDAY!"

Now present your own conversations.

Functions

Greeting People

Hello.
[less formal]
Hi.
[more formal]
How do you do?

(It's) nice to meet you.
(It's) nice meeting you.
(I'm) happy to meet you.
(I'm) glad to meet you.
(I'm) pleased to meet you.

How are you?
How have you been?
[less formal]
How are you doing?
How are things?
How's it going?
   Fine (thank you/thanks).
   Good.
   All right.
   Okay.
   Not bad.

Introductions

Introducing Oneself

My name is _____.
I'm _____.

Introducing Others

Let me introduce (you to) _____.
I'd like to introduce (you to) _____.
I'd like you to meet _____.
[less formal]
Meet _____.
This is _____.

Identifying

My friend *Paul*, my brother *Tom*, . . .

She's the one who _____.

Apologizing

I'm sorry.
Excuse me.

Asking for and Reporting Information

Where are you from?
   Japan.
What do you do?
   I'm an *English teacher.*
Which *apartment do you live in?*
How long *have you been studying here?*
Who *is your doctor?*
Whose *family are you in?*
What kind of *music do you play?*
When *are you due?*

How about you?
What about you?
And you?

Don't you work at the bank on Main
   Street?

How is she?
   Pretty good.
   Fine.
   She looks terrific/great/fine.

Did _____ have anything to say?

Conversation Strategies

Initiating Conversations

I don't think we've met.

Excuse me, but . . .
Pardon me, but . . .

Don't I know you from somewhere?

Initiating a Topic

Guess _____!
You won't believe _____!

Asking for and Reporting
 Information
Asking for and Reporting
 Additional Information
Describing
Congratulating
Sympathizing

Hesitating
Initiating a Topic

Good News!
Bad News!
Have You Heard from . . .?
What Do They Look Like?
What Are They Like?
Tell Me a Little About Yourself

• Adjectives • Must • Passives • Possessive Adjectives
• Pronouns • Simple Present Tense • Tense Review

Good News!

A. I have some good news.
B. Really? What is it?
A. I was just promoted to assistant manager!
B. Assistant manager?! **That's fantastic!**(1)
You must be **thrilled.**(2)
A. I am.
B. Well, congratulations! **I'm very happy to hear that.**(3)
A. Thanks.

1. given a twenty percent raise

2. accepted at Oxford University

3. awarded the Nobel Prize for Physics

4. named "Outstanding Employee of the Year"

5. offered a movie contract by a major Hollywood studio

Now present your own conversations.

Bad News!

A. I have some bad news.
B. Oh? What is it?
A. My husband just lost his job.
B. He did?
A. I'm afraid so.
B. Oh, **that's too bad!**[1] You must be very upset.
A. I am.
B. **I'm very sorry to hear about that.**[2]

[1] That's too bad!
That's a shame/a pity!
What a shame/a pity!

[2] I'm (very) sorry to hear (about) that.
I'm (very/so) sorry.

1. My dog was run over by a car.

2. The factory where I work is going to shut down next month.

3. My son and his wife have decided to get a divorce.

4. I have to stay home all weekend and take care of my little brother.

5. I was rejected by every medical school I applied to.

Now present your own conversations.

Have You Heard from . . .?

A. Have you **heard from**[1] your granddaughter lately?
B. As a matter of fact, I have. I **heard from**[1] her just the other day.
A. **How's she doing?**[2]
B. **Fine.**[3] She's getting straight A's in school.
A. She is? That's fantastic!
B. I think so, too.
A. Next time you see her, please **give her my regards.**[4]
B. I'll be sure to do that.

A. Have you **run into**[1] your cousin Ralph lately?
B. As a matter of fact, I have. I **ran into**[1] him just the other day.
A. **How's he doing?**[2]
B. **Not too well.**[5] He had to have four teeth pulled last week.
A. He did? That's too bad!
B. I think so, too.
A. Next time you see him, please **tell him I'm thinking of him.**[4]
B. I'll be sure to do that.

[1] heard from run into talked to seen spoken to been in touch with	[2] How's she doing? How is she? How has she been?	[3] Fine. Great. Wonderful.	[4] give her my regards tell her I say/said hello tell her I'm thinking of her
	[5] Not too well. Not so well. Not very well.		

1. your parents

2. your neighbors across the street

3. your son

4. your cousins in Detroit

5. George and Irene

6. Janet

7. your friend Elizabeth

8. your grandfather

9. The President

*Parent Teacher Association

Now present your own conversations.

What Do They Look Like?

A. Could you please take these reports over to Charlie Jones in Accounting?
B. Sure. I'd be happy to. But I'm afraid I don't remember what he looks like.
A. Oh, you can't miss him. He's **about your height**, **sort of heavy**, with **curly dark** hair.
B. Okay. I think I'll be able to find him.
A. Thanks very much. I appreciate it.

height	weight	hair		additional features
about your height	sort of	curly	dark	and (wears) glasses
about average height	kind of } heavy/thin	wavy	light	and (has) a beard/
about ___ feet tall	very	straight	brown	mustache
(very) tall	a little on the		black	
(very) short	heavy side		blond(e)	
a little taller/shorter			red	
than you/me			gray	

Complete these conversations using the information above.

1. Could you please take these boxes over to Stella in Shipping?

2. Would you be willing to pick up my brother at the airport?

3. Could you possibly get some chalk from Ms. Crenshaw in the principal's office?

4. Could I possibly ask you to meet my sister at the train station?

5. Could I possibly ask you to take another picture of my Uncle Charlie?

"WHAT DO THEY LOOK LIKE?"

Now present your own conversations.

What Are They Like?

A. **Have you heard anything**(1) about our new English teacher?
B. Yes. **People say**(2) she's very intelligent.
A. Hmm. **What else have you heard?**(3)
B. Well, they also say she's very patient.
A. Really? That's interesting.

(1)	Have you heard anything Do you know anything
(2)	People say They say People/They tell me Everybody says Everybody tells me I've heard Word has it (that)
(3)	What else have you heard? Have you heard anything else? Do you know anything else?

1. the new boss
bright
strict

2. the new superintendent
friendly
helpful

3. the new student in our class
nice
outgoing

4. our new senator
articulate
honest

5. the new supervisor
unfriendly
short-tempered

Now present your own conversations.

Tell Me a Little About Yourself

(1) I don't know where to
     begin.
     I don't know where to start.
     I don't know what to say.

(2) What do you want to know?
     What would you like to
        know?
     What can I tell you?

(3) exciting
     interesting
     challenging
     difficult
     important
     creative
     ·
     ·
     ·

A. So, tell me a little about yourself.
B. Gee - uh . . . **I don't know where to begin.**(1)
    What do you want to know?(2)
A. Well, let's see . . . What do you do?
B. I'm a civil engineer.
A. A civil engineer. Hmm. That's interesting.
    Do you enjoy your work?
B. Yes. I like it a lot.
A. Tell me, what exactly do you do as a civil engineer?
B. Well, I design roads and bridges for the city.
A. Oh. That sounds like a very **exciting**(3) job.
B. It is.

1. I'm a criminal lawyer.
    I defend people accused of crimes.

2. I'm a political speech writer.
    I write speeches for a congressman.

3. I'm an administrative assistant.
I handle all the business communication
for the president of my company.

4. I'm an emergency medical technician.
I drive an ambulance and assist
people with medical emergencies.

5. I'm a real estate agent.
I help people who want to buy or sell
a house.

6. I'm an anthropologist.
I study about people from different
cultures all over the world.

7. I'm a computer programmer.
I design computer programs for
business and industry.

8. I'm a meteorologist.
I report the weather on TV.

9. I'm a forest ranger.
I watch out for fires and protect all
the animals in the forest.

"TELL ME A LITTLE ABOUT YOURSELF"

Now present your own conversations.

Functions

Asking for and Reporting Information

Have you { heard from / run into / talked to / seen / spoken to / been in touch with } ___ lately?

How's _____ doing?
How is _____?
How has _____ been?
   Fine.
   Great.
   Wonderful.
   Not too well.
   Not so well.
   Not very well.

Have you heard anything about _____?
Do you know anything about ____?

People say . . .
They say . . .
People/They tell me . . .
Everybody says . . .
Everybody tells me . . .
I've heard . . .
Word has it (that) . . .

Tell me a little about yourself.

What do you want to know?
What would you like to know?
What can I tell you?

Asking for and Reporting Additional Information

What else have you heard?
Have you heard anything else?
Do you know anything else?

Describing

He's about your height, sort of heavy, with curly dark hair.

He's/She's very _____.

Congratulating

That's fantastic!
That's great/wonderful/exciting/marvelous!

Congratulations!

I'm very happy to hear that.
I'm very happy for you.

Sympathizing

That's too bad!
That's a shame/a pity!
What a shame/a pity!

I'm (very) sorry to hear (about) that.
I'm (very/so) sorry.

Requests

Direct, More Polite

Could you please _____?
Could you possibly _____?
Could I possibly ask you to _____?
Would you be willing to _____?

Surprise-Disbelief

Assistant manager?!

Deduction

You must be _____.

Conversation Strategies

Hesitating

Gee-uh . . .

I don't know where to begin.
I don't know where to start.
I don't know what to say.

Well, let's see . . .

Initiating a Topic

I have some good/bad news.

Asking for and Reporting
  Information
Asking for and Reporting
  Additional Information
Describing
Identifying
Certainty/Uncertainty
Remembering/Forgetting

Focusing Attention
Initiating a Topic

Which One?
What's It Like There?
As Far As I Know . . .
Did You Remember?
Did You Hear?
Have You Heard the News?
What Happened?

• Adjectives • Declarative Sentences with Question
Intonation • Embedded Questions • Indirect Objects
• One/Ones • Passives • Past Continuous Tense • Past
Tense • Sequence of Tenses • Superlatives • Tag
Questions

Which One?

> You should wear your new tie with that jacket.

(1) You should wear _____.
Why don't you wear_____?
How about wearing _____?

The children gave you a *blue* tie *with gray and yellow stripes.*

A. **You should wear**(1) your new tie with that jacket.
B. Which one?
A. The one the children gave you.
B. Hmm. Which one is that?
A. You remember. It's the *blue* one *with gray and yellow stripes.*
B. Oh, that one. I know where it is. I'll get it.

> Why don't you wear your new bathing suit to the beach?

1. I gave you a *purple* bathing suit *with yellow polka dots.*

> How about wearing your new sweater this evening?

2. Aunt Margaret sent you a *wool* sweater *made in Scotland.*

> You should wear that pretty scarf of yours.

3. The people at the office gave you a *red* scarf *made of silk.*

> Let's take the camera with us!

4. Uncle Harry gave us a *pocket-size* camera *in a brown leather case.*

> Why don't you play with your new doll?

5. Grandma sent you a *cute* doll *that cries when you pull the string.*

"WHICH ONE?"

Now present your own conversations.

What's It Like There?

A. Have you by any chance ever been to Hong Kong?
B. Yes, I have. Why?
A. I'm going there with my family for a vacation next month. Can you tell me what it's like there?
B. Well, it's a very *exciting* place. **As a matter of fact,**[1] it's probably one of the *most exciting* places I know.
A. Really? That's good to hear. **Can you tell me anything else?**[2]
B. Well-uh . . . what else would you like to know?
A. How about the weather . . . and the people?
B. The weather at this time of year is usually *cool*, and **in my opinion,**[3] the people there are very *interesting*.
A. It sounds like a wonderful place.
B. It is. I'm sure you'll have a good time there.

[1] As a matter of fact,
    In fact,

[2] Can you tell me anything else?
    Can you tell me anything more?
    What else can you tell me?

[3] in my opinion,
    if you ask me,
    as far as I'm concerned,

1. dynamic
warm
nice

2. nice
pleasant
easygoing

3. pretty
delightful
pleasant

4. charming
cool
helpful

5. lively
comfortable
friendly

"WHAT'S IT LIKE THERE?"

Now present your own conversations.

As Far As I Know . . .

When is the President going to arrive?

(1) Do you/Would you (by any chance) know
Do you/Would you (by any chance) happen to know

(2) I don't think so.
Not as far as I know.

(3) Are you sure/certain/positive (about that)?

(4) I'm positive/certain/sure.
I'm absolutely positive/certain/sure.
I'm a hundred percent sure.
There's no doubt about it.

A. **Do you by any chance know**[1] when the President is going to arrive?
B. Yes. As far as I know, he's going to arrive at 2:30.
A. Hmm. Somehow I thought he was going to arrive earlier than that.
B. **I don't think so.**[2]
A. **Are you sure?**[3]
B. Yes, **I'm positive.**[4] He arrives at 2:30.

When does the post office open?

1. at 9

What time does the bank close?

2. at 4

What time does the movie begin?

3. at 7:45

When is Nancy due?

4. late next month

When is your mother planning to leave?

5. two weeks from Sunday

"AS FAR AS I KNOW..."

Now present your own conversations.

22

Did You Remember?

A. Uh-oh! **Did you remember to**[(1)] feed the dog?
B. No, I didn't. I thought YOU were going to feed him!
A. Hmm. I guess I WAS . . . but **I forgot all about it.**[(2)]
B. Well, since the dog hasn't been fed yet, I guess one of us should go and do it.
A. Okay. I'll do it.

[(1)] Did you (happen to) remember to _____?
You didn't (by any chance) remember to _____, did you?

[(2)] I forgot (all about it).
I completely forgot.
It (completely) slipped my mind.

1. take the garbage out

2. set the table

3. turn the downstairs lights off

4. do the laundry

5. change the baby's diaper

Now present your own conversations.

Did You Hear?

School is going to be closed tomorrow!

A. Did you hear (that) school is going to be closed tomorrow?
B. **You're kidding!**[1] School isn't really going to be closed tomorrow, is it?
A. Yes, it is.
B. Are you sure?
A. I'm absolutely positive! I heard it on the radio.

1. I saw it in the paper.

They predict a hurricane for tomorrow!

2. I heard it on TV.

We won five gold medals at the Olympics today!

3. I heard it on the radio.

4. I read it in the morning paper.

The Americans and the Russians have just signed a nuclear arms treaty!

5. I heard it on the 7 o'clock news.

"DID YOU HEAR?"

Now present your own conversations.

Have You Heard the News?

A. Have you heard the news?
B. No, what?
A. They're going to make the park across the street into a parking lot.
B. They're going to make the park across the street into a parking lot?! I don't believe it! **Where did you hear that?**(1)
A. All the neighbors are talking about it.
B. Do you think it's true?
A. I think so, but **I don't know for sure.**(2)
B. Well, personally, I doubt it.

(1) Where did you hear that?
How do you know (that)?
Who told you (that)?

(2) I don't know for sure.
I'm not (completely/absolutely) positive.
I'm not a hundred percent positive.

1. It's a rumor going around town.

2. I heard it from some people at the supermarket.

3. I overheard some people talking on the bus.

4. It's a rumor going around the office.

5. Some kids in my class were talking about it.

Now present your own conversations.

INTERCHANGE
What Happened?

A. What happened?
B. Well, I was lying on the beach listening to the radio, when suddenly I heard someone shouting for help.
A. So what did you do?
B. I jumped up, looked out toward the ocean, and saw a little boy waving his arms in the air.
A. **What did you do next?**[1]
B. I took off my shirt and my watch and jumped into the water.
A. **And THEN what did you do?**[1]
B. I swam out to the little boy, held him so his head stayed above water, and brought him back to shore.
A. Well, that sounds like it was quite an experience!
B. It sure was!

A. What happened?
B. Well, I was _____ing, when suddenly _____.
A. So what did you do?
B. _____.
A. **What did you do next?**[1]
B. _____.
A. **And THEN what did you do?**[1]
B. _____.
A. Well, that sounds like it was quite an experience!
B. It sure was!

---

[1]   What did you do next?   And then what did you do?
      What did you do after that?   What was the next thing you did?

1.

2.

You're telling somebody about something that happened. Create an original conversation using the model dialog on p. 26 as a guide. Feel free to adapt and expand the model any way you wish.

Functions

Asking for and Reporting Information

Which one is that?

Have you by any chance ever _____ed?

Can you tell me what it's like?

Do you/Would you (by any chance) know _____?
Do you/Would you (by any chance) happen to know _____?

Did you hear (that) _____?

What happened?

Where did you hear that?
How do you know (that)?
Who told you (that)?

I heard it on the radio/on TV/on the news.
I saw/read it in the paper.

School isn't really going to be closed tomorrow, is it?

Asking for and Reporting Additional Information

Can you tell me anything else?
Can you tell me anything more?
What else can you tell me?

What did you do next?
What did you do after that?
And then what did you do?
What was the next thing you did?

What else would you like to know?

As a matter of fact, . . .
In fact, . . .

Describing

It's the _____ one with the _____.

It's a (very) _____ _____.

It's one of the _____est _____s I know.

Identifying

The one *the children gave you.*

Certainty/Uncertainty

Inquiring about . . .

Are you positive/certain/sure (about that)?

Expressing Certainty

I'm positive/certain/sure.
I'm absolutely positive/certain/sure.
I'm a hundred percent sure.
There's no doubt about it.
I'm absolutely positive.

Expressing Uncertainty

I don't know for sure.
I'm not (completely/absolutely) positive.
I'm not a hundred percent positive.

I don't think so.
Not as far as I know.

I doubt it.

Remembering/Forgetting

Inquiring about . . .

Did you (happen to) remember to _____?
You didn't (by any chance) remember to _____, did you?

Indicating . . .

I forgot (all about it).
I completely forgot.
It (completely) slipped my mind.

You remember.

Oh, that one.

Surprise-Disbelief

School isn't really going to be closed tomorrow, is it?

They're going to make the park across the street into a parking lot?!

You're kidding!
No kidding!
You're joking!
I don't/can't believe it!
Oh, come on!
No!
That can't be!
You've got to be kidding!

Advice-Suggestions

Offering . . .

You should _____.
Why don't you _____?
How about _____ing?

Conversation Strategies

Focusing Attention

As a matter of fact, . . .
In fact, . . .

In my opinion, . . .
If you ask me, . . .
As far as I'm concerned, . . .

Initiating a Topic

Have you heard the news?

Who do you think these people are?
What do you think they're talking about?
Create conversations based on these scenes and act them out.

1.

2.

3.

4.

5.

6.

7.

8.

What Did You Say?
I'm Sorry. I Didn't Hear You
Have You Got It?
Are You With Me So Far?

• Embedded Questions • Gerunds • Imperatives
• Partitives • Question Formation • Sequence of Tenses

What Did You Say?

A. Would you mind playing your radio someplace else?
B. I'm sorry. **I didn't hear you.**[1] **What did you say?**[2]
A. I asked you if you'd play your radio someplace else.
B. Sure. I'd be happy to.
A. Thanks.

1.

2.

3.

4.

5.

Now present your own conversations.

I'm Sorry. I Didn't Hear You

(1) WHEN do you want me to
WHEN should I
WHEN did you tell me to

A. Please report for work tomorrow at 7:45.
B. I'm sorry. I didn't hear you.
WHEN do you want me to(1) report for work tomorrow?
A. At 7:45.
B. Oh, okay.

1. Please give these
packages to Tom.

2. Please get a loaf of bread
and a dozen eggs at the
supermarket.

3. Put three slices of tomato
on each salad.

4. Take these pills four
times a day.

5. Put the money in a
brown paper bag.

Now present your own
conversations.

Have You Got It?

Speech bubble:
- *Go to the corner and turn right.*
- *Walk two blocks to Main Street.*
- *Turn left, walk two more blocks, and you'll see the post office next to the bank.*

A. **Could you please tell me**[(1)] how to get to the post office?
B. Sure. Go to the corner and turn right. Walk two blocks to Main Street. Turn left, walk two more blocks, and you'll see the post office next to the bank. **Have you got it?**[(2)]
A. I think so. **Let me see.**[(3)]
   First, I go to the corner and turn right.
B. **Uh-húh.**[(4)]
A. Then I walk two blocks to Main Street. Right?
B. **Um-hḿm.**[(4)]
A. And then I . . . Hmm. I forgot the last part. What do I do after that?
B. You turn left, walk two more blocks, and you'll see the post office next to the bank.
A. Okay.
B. Do you think you've got it now?
A. I think so. Thanks very much.

[(1)] Could you (please/possibly) tell me
Do you/Would you (by any chance) know
Can you (please) tell me
Would you (possibly/by any chance) be able to tell me

[(2)] (Have you) got it?
Do you follow me?
Okay?

[(3)] Let me see.
Let me see if I understand.
Let me see if I've got that (right).

[(4)] Uh-húh.
Um-hḿm.
Yes.
(That's) right.

34

A. **Could you please tell me**[1] how to _____?
B. Sure. _____.
   _____
   _____.

Have you got it?[2]
A. I think so. **Let me see.**[3]
   First, I _____.
B. **Uh-húh.**[4]
A. Then I _____. Right?
B. **Um-hḿm.**[4]
A. And then I . . . Hmm. I forgot the last part. What do I do after that?
B. You _____
A. Okay.
B. Do you think you've got it now?
A. I think so. Thanks very much.

• *Pick up the receiver.*

• *Put in the money.*

• *Wait for the dial tone and dial.*

1. use this telephone

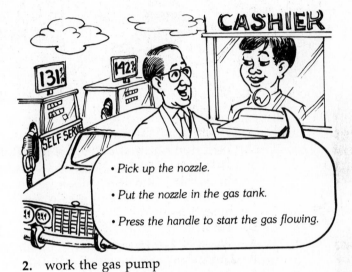

• *Pick up the nozzle.*

• *Put the nozzle in the gas tank.*

• *Press the handle to start the gas flowing.*

2. work the gas pump

• *Use the jack to raise up the car.*

• *Unscrew the bolts and take off the flat tire.*

• *Put on the new tire, put the bolts on tight, and lower the car.*

3. change a flat tire

• *Turn around and drive down this road until you get to a big intersection.*

• *Take a left and drive about three miles until you get to the entrance of the interstate.*

• *Take the interstate north to exit 27.*

4. get to the airport

Now present your own conversations.

INTERCHANGE
Are You With Me So Far?

A. Could you tell me your recipe for chocolate chip cookies?
B. Sure. I'll be happy to. But it's pretty complicated. You might want to write this down.
A. I'm afraid I don't have a pencil on me. But go ahead anyway.
B. Okay. First, mix together 2 cups of flour and a teaspoon of baking soda. Then, add a teaspoon of salt. After that, mix together a cup of butter and a cup of sugar in a separate bowl. **Are you with me so far?**[1]
A. Yes, I'm with you.
B. Okay. Then, add 2 eggs. Next, combine all the ingredients into a large bowl. And then . . .
A. Wait a minute! **I didn't get that.**[2] Could you repeat the last two **instructions?**[3]
B. Sure. Add 2 eggs. And combine all the ingredients into a large bowl.
A. Okay. **Now I've got it.**[4]
B. Good. Now, let's see. Where was I? Oh, yes. Slowly mix in a cup of chocolate chips and a cup of nuts. Then, form little cookies from the mixture and place them on a cookie sheet. And finally, bake for 8 minutes at 375 degrees Fahrenheit. Have you got all that?
A. I think so. But let me repeat that back to make sure. First, I . . .

---

[1] Are you with me (so far)?
Okay (so far)?
Are you following me (so far)?

[2] I didn't get that.
I'm lost.
I'm not following you.

[3] instructions
directions
steps
things you said

[4] Now I've got it.
I understand.
I see.
I'm with you.

A. Could you tell me _____?
B. Sure. I'll be happy to. But it's pretty complicated. You might want to write this down.
A. I'm afraid I don't have a pencil on me. But go ahead anyway.
B. Okay. First, _____.
   Then, _____.
   After that, _____.
   Are you with me so far?[1]
A. Yes, I'm with you.
B. Okay. Then, _____.
   Next, _____.
   And then . . .
A. Wait a minute! **I didn't get that.**[2] Could you repeat the last two **instructions?**[3]
B. Sure. _____.
   And _____.
A. Okay. **Now I've got it.**[4]
B. Good. Now, let's see. Where was I? Oh, yes.
   _____.
   Then, _____.
   And finally, _____.
   Have you got all that?
A. I think so. But let me repeat that back to make sure.
   First, I . . .

Write out a list of 8 steps to do something. (For example, directions to a place, how to make or repair something, or a recipe.)

1. _____
2. _____
3. _____
4. _____
5. _____
6. _____
7. _____
8. _____

Create an original conversation using your list of instructions and the model dialog above as a guide. (Be sure to have the other person repeat back your instructions to make sure he or she understands you.) Feel free to adapt and expand the model any way you wish.

Functions

Instructing

(Please) _____.

First, . . .
Then, . . .
After that, . . .
Next, . . .
And finally, . . .

Directions-Location

Giving Directions

Go to _____.
Turn _____.
Walk _____ blocks.

Asking for and Reporting Information

Could you (please/possibly) tell me
_____?
Do you/Would you (by any chance)
know _____?
Can you (please) tell me _____?
Would you (possibly/by any chance)
be able to tell me_____?

Requests

Direct, Polite

Please _____.

Direct, More Polite

Would you mind _____ing?

Conversation Strategies

Asking for Repetition

I didn't hear you.
I didn't (quite) catch that.
I didn't get that.
I missed that.
I'm lost.
I'm not following you.

What did you say?
Could/Would you (please) repeat
   that?
Could/Would you say that again?
Would you mind saying that again?
Would you mind repeating that?

Could you repeat the last two $\begin{cases} \text{instructions?} \\ \text{directions?} \\ \text{steps?} \\ \text{things you said?} \end{cases}$

WHEN do you want me to _____?
WHEN should I _____?
WHEN did you tell me to _____?

I forgot the last part.

Checking and Indicating Understanding

Checking Another Person's Understanding

(Have you) got it?
Do you follow me?
Okay?

Are you with me (so far)?
Okay (so far)?
Are you following me (so far)?

Do you think you've got it now?
Have you got all that?

Checking One's Own Understanding

Let me see.
Let me see if I understand.
Let me see if I've got that (right).
Let me repeat that back.

Indicating Understanding

Now I've got it.
I understand.
I see.
I'm with you.

Uh-húh.
Um-hḿm.
Yes.
(That's) right.

**Satisfaction/Dissatis-
faction
Likes/Dislikes
Complimenting
Disappointment
Complaining
Advice-Suggestions**

Thanks for Saying So
You're Just Saying That!
Just What I Had in Mind!
I'd Like a Refund, Please
I Was a Little Disappointed
I'm Really Annoyed
Would You Like to Get Together This Weekend?

• Adjectives • Comparatives • Gerunds • Infinitives
• Negative Questions • Present Continuous Tense to
Express Habitual Action • Singular/Plural • Superlatives
• Too/Enough • Would

Thanks for Saying So

(1) a very good
quite a

[less formal]
some

(2) Yes.
Absolutely.

(3) excellent
wonderful
terrific
magnificent
fabulous
superb

(4) Thanks/Thank you (for saying so).
It's nice of you to say so/that.

A. That was **a very good**(1) performance!
B. Did you really like it?
A. **Yes.**(2) I thought it was **excellent.**(3)
B. **Thanks for saying so.**(4)

1. dinner

2. lecture

3. presentation

4. party

5. speech

Now present your own conversations.

You're Just Saying That!

A. I **really like**(1) your apartment. It's **very**(2) spacious.
B. **Oh, go on!**(3) You're just saying that!
A. No. **I mean it!**(4) It's one of the most spacious apartments I've ever seen.
B. Well, thanks for saying so. I'm glad you like it.

(1) (really) like
     love

(2) very
     so

(3) Oh/Aw, go on!
     Oh/Aw, come on!
     Oh!

(4) I mean it!
     I'm (really) serious.
     I'm being honest with you.

1. tie
     attractive

2. dress
     pretty

3. painting
     interesting

4. blouse
     colorful

5. haircut
     nice

Now present your own conversations.

Just What I Had in Mind!

(1)	How do you like
	What do you think of
(2)	fine
	very nice
	perfect
(3)	satisfied
	happy
	pleased
(4)	Very.
	Very much.
	Yes.
(5)	just what I
	had in mind/
	wanted/was
	looking for

A. **How do you like**[1] the bicycle?
B. It's **fine.**[2]
A. It isn't too heavy?
B. No, not at all.
A. Is it large enough?
B. Oh, yes. I wouldn't want it any larger.
A. So you're **satisfied**[3] with it?
B. **Very.**[4] It's **just what I had in mind!**[5]

1. mattress
   short
   firm

2. tennis racket
   big
   light

3. wedding dress
   plain
   fancy

4. pants
   tight
   long

5. gloves
   bulky
   warm

Now present your own conversations.

I'd Like a Refund, Please

A. I'd like to return this hat.
B. **What seems to be the problem with it?**[1]
A. It's too old-fashioned.
B. Would you like to exchange it for one that's more modern?
A. **I don't think so.**[2] I'd just like a refund, please.
B. I'm sorry. We don't give refunds. **However,**[3] we'll be happy to offer you credit toward another purchase in our store.
A. No refunds??
B. I'm afraid not.
A. Oh. Thanks anyway.

[1] What seems to be the problem (with it)?
What seems to be the matter (with it)?
What's the problem/the matter/wrong (with it)?

[2] I don't think so.
Not really.
Probably not.

[3] However,
But

1. coat
   long
   short

2. sport shirt
   flashy
   conservative

3. Home Repair book
   complicated
   simple

4. video game
   easy
   challenging

5. parrot
   talkative
   quiet

Now present your own conversations.

I Was a Little Disappointed

A. How did you like the play?
B. Well, **to tell the truth,**(1) **I was a little disappointed.**(2)
A. **Why?**(3)
B. It wasn't as funny as I thought it would be.
   I really **expected it to be**(4) a lot funnier.
A. That's too bad.

1. your vacation
   relaxing

2. the game
   exciting

3. the steak
   juicy

4. your date with Ted last night
   enjoyable

5. English class today
   good

Now present your own
conversations.

I'm Really Annoyed

A. I'm really **annoyed with**(1) my landlord.
B. Why?
A. **He's always**(2) forgetting to fix things.
B. Have you spoken to him about it?
A. Well, actually not.
B. I don't understand. If his forgetting to fix things **bothers**(3) you so much, why don't you **mention it to him?**(4)
A. I guess I should. But I don't like to complain.

(1) annoyed with
upset with

[stronger]
mad at
angry at
furious with

(2) He's always
He's constantly
He keeps on

(3) bothers
annoys
upsets

(4) mention it to him
talk to him about it
discuss it with him
bring up the subject
   with him

1. My secretary is always making spelling mistakes.

2. My neighbors are always playing their stereo past midnight.

3. My teacher is always giving us homework over the weekend.

4. My roommate is always snoring at night.

5. My parents are always treating me like a baby.

Now present your own conversations.

INTERCHANGE
Would You Like to Get Together This Weekend?

A. Would you like to get together this weekend?
B. Sure. What would you like to do?
A. Well, how about seeing a movie?
B. That sounds good. Did you have any particular movie in mind?
A. Well, they say that "A Man and His Horse" is very good. It's playing at the Rialto Theater.
B. "A Man and His Horse"? That's a **western**,[1] isn't it?
A. I think so.
B. Well, to tell the truth, **I don't like westerns**[1] **very much.**[2]
A. Oh. Well, is there any particular movie you'd like to see?
B. How about "The Return of the Monster"? It's playing at the Shopping Mall Cinema, and I hear it's excellent.
A. "Return of the Monster"? Hmm. Isn't that a **science fiction movie?**[1]
B. Yes. Don't you like **science fiction movies?**[1]
A. No, not really. Maybe we shouldn't see a movie. Maybe we should do something else.
B. Okay. Would you be interested in doing something outdoors?
A. Sure. Any suggestions?
B. Well, we could go ice skating.
A. Oh. I'm afraid **I don't really enjoy**[2] going ice skating. How about going hiking?
B. Well, to tell the truth, I've gone hiking several times in the past few weeks.
A. Really? Then I guess you must be pretty **tired of**[3] hiking.
B. I am. Let's do something else.
A. Why don't we just have dinner together somewhere this Saturday?
B. That sounds like a good idea. Where would you like to go?
A. Well, one of my favorite places to eat is "The Captain's Table."
B. Hmm. "The Captain's Table"? What kind of food do they serve there?
A. **Seafood.**[4] But if you don't like **seafood,**[4] we can go someplace else.
B. No. On the contrary, I LOVE **seafood!**[4]
A. You do?! Great!
B. Then **it's settled.**[5] "The Captain's Table" for dinner on Saturday. What time?
A. How about 7 o'clock?
B. Is 8 okay?
A. Fine.

(1)
western	adventure movie	foreign film
comedy	science fiction movie	cartoon
mystery	documentary	tear-jerker
drama	children's film	pornographic movie

(2)
I don't (really) like/enjoy _____ very much.

I don't (particularly) care for _____.

I'm not (really) crazy about _____.

[stronger]
I hate _____.

(3)
tired of
sick of
sick and tired of

(4)
seafood
steak and potatoes
pizza
fried chicken
vegetarian food
American food
Chinese food

(5)
It's settled.
We're set.
We're agreed.

A. Would you like to get together this weekend?
B. Sure. What would you like to do?
A. Well, how about seeing a movie?
B. That sounds good. Did you have any particular movie in mind?
A. Well, they say that "_____" is very good. It's playing at the _____.
B. "_____"? That's a _____,(1) isn't it?
A. I think so.
B. Well, to tell the truth, **I don't like** _____s(1) **very much.**(2)
A. Oh. Well, is there any particular movie you'd like to see?
B. How about "_____"? It's playing at the _____, and I hear it's excellent.
A. "_____"? Hmm. Isn't that a _____?(1)
B. Yes. Don't you like _____s?(1)
A. No, not really. Maybe we shouldn't see a movie. Maybe we should do something else.
B. Okay. Would you be interested in doing something outdoors?
A. Sure. Any suggestions?
B. Well, we could go _____ing.
A. Oh. I'm afraid **I don't really enjoy**(2) going _____ing. How about going _____ing?
B. Well, to tell the truth, I've gone _____ing several times in the past few weeks.
A. Really? Then I guess you must be pretty **tired of**(3) _____ing.
B. I am. Let's do something else.
A. Why don't we just have dinner together somewhere this Saturday?
B. That sounds like a good idea. Where would you like to go?
A. Well, one of my favorite places to eat is "_____."
B. Hmm. "_____"? What kind of food do they serve there?
A. _____.(4) But if you don't like _____,(4) we can go someplace else.
B. No. On the contrary, I LOVE _____!(4)
A. You do?! Great!
B. Then **it's settled.**(5) "_____" for dinner on Saturday. What time?
A. How about _____ o'clock?
B. Is _____ okay?
A. Fine.

Create an original conversation using the model dialog above as a guide. In your conversation, use the names of movies, theaters, and restaurants where you live, and refer to outdoor activities you enjoy doing on the weekend. Feel free to adapt and expand the model any way you wish.

Functions

Satisfaction/Dissatisfaction

Inquiring about . . .

How do you like _____?
What do you think of _____?

How did you like _____?

Did you (really) like it?

Are you { satisfied / happy / pleased } with it?

Is it _____ enough?

What seems to be the problem (with it)?
What seems to be the matter (with it)?
What's the problem/the matter/ wrong (with it)?

Expressing Satisfaction

It's { fine. / very nice. / perfect. }

It's just what I { had in mind. / wanted. / was looking for. }

I wouldn't want it any _____er.

Expressing Dissatisfaction

It's too _____.

I really { expected it to be / thought it would be / hoped it would be } _____er.

It wasn't as _____ as I thought it would be.

Gratitude

Expressing . . .

Thanks/Thank you (for saying so).
It's nice of you to say so/that.

Persuading-Insisting

I mean it!
I'm (really) serious.
I'm being honest with you.

Likes/Dislikes

Inquiring about . . .

How do you like _____?
What do you think of _____?

How did you like _____?

Did you like _____?

Don't you like _____?

Expressing Likes

I like _____.
I love _____.

Expressing Dislikes

I don't (really) like/enjoy _____ very much.
I don't (particularly) care for _____.

I'm not (really) crazy about _____.

[stronger]
I hate _____.

Complimenting

Expressing Compliments

That was { a very good / quite a / [less formal] / some } _____!

I thought it was { excellent. / wonderful. / terrific. / magnificent. / fabulous. / superb. }

I (really) like _____.
I love _____.

It's very _____.
It's so _____.

It's one of the _____est _____s
I've ever _____ed.

Responding to Compliments

Thanks/Thank you (for saying so).
It's nice of you to say so/that.
I'm glad you like it.

Oh/Aw, go on!
Oh/Aw, come on!
Oh!

You're just saying that.

Disappointment

I was (a little) disappointed.
I wasn't very pleased with it.
It was (a little) disappointing.

Complaining

It's too _____.

I was (a little) disappointed.
I wasn't very pleased with it.
It was (a little) disappointing.

I'm { annoyed with / upset with / [stronger] / mad at / angry at / furious with } _____.

He's always
He's constantly } _____ing.
He keeps on

His _____ing { bothers / annoys / upsets } me.

I'm tired of _____(ing).
I'm sick of _____(ing).
I'm sick and tired of _____(ing).

Advice-Suggestions

Asking for . . .

Any suggestions?

Offering . . .

How about _____?
How about _____ing?
Would you be interested in _____?
We could _____.
Why don't we _____?
Let's _____.

Why don't you _____?

Have you _____ed?

Maybe we should _____.
Maybe we shouldn't _____.

They say that _____ is very good.
One of my favorite _____s is _____.

Is _____ okay?

I'd Prefer a Baked Potato
I'd Much Rather See a Movie
A Serious Disagreement
It Doesn't Make Any Difference
It's Entirely Up to You
The International Gourmet

• Gerunds • Infinitives • Partitives • Present Perfect Tense
• Sequence of Tenses • Want + Object + Infinitive
• Whether • WH-ever Words • Would

I'd Prefer a Baked Potato

(1) I'd like
I'll have
I want

(2) prefer
rather have
like

a steak
rare
a baked potato
a cup of coffee

A. May I help you?
B. Yes, **I'd like**(1) a steak.
A. How would you like it?
B. Rare.
A. Okay. And would you **prefer**(2) a baked potato or rice with that?
B. I'd **prefer**(2) a baked potato.
A. Anything to drink?
B. How about a cup of coffee, please?
A. Okay. That's a rare steak with a baked potato and a cup of coffee.

a hamburger
well-done
french fries
a Coke

1. french fries or potato chips?

the chicken
baked
a salad
a glass of white wine

2. a salad or a vegetable?

an order of eggs
scrambled
toast
a glass of milk

3. toast or a muffin?

a cheese sandwich
grilled
potato salad
a glass of lemonade

4. potato salad or cole slaw?

the fish
fried
noodles
a diet soda

5. noodles or mashed potatoes?

"I'D PREFER A BAKED POTATO"

Now present your own conversations.

I'd Much Rather See a Movie

A. **Would you like to**(1) stay home or see a movie?
B. I think **I'd prefer to**(2) stay home. How about you?
A. Well, to be honest, **I really don't feel like** staying home.(3)
   I'd much rather see a movie. Is that okay with you?
B. Sure. We haven't seen a movie in a long time anyway.

(1) Would you like to
    Would you prefer to
    Would you rather
    Do you want to

(2) I'd prefer to
    I'd rather
    I'd like to

(3) I (really) don't feel like
    _____ing.
    I'm not (really) in the mood
    to _____.
    I'd (really) prefer not to
    _____.

1. eat at home or at a restaurant?

2. swim at the beach or in the pool?

3. walk home or take a taxi?

4. watch the game on TV or go to the stadium?

5. put Rover in the kennel or take him on vacation with us?

"I'D MUCH RATHER SEE A MOVIE"

Now present your own conversations.

A Serious Disagreement

I want you to switch to the night shift.

I'd rather stay on the day shift.

A. **You've seemed troubled**[1] for the past few days. Is anything **wrong?**[2]
B. Well, to tell the truth, I've been having a disagreement with my boss.
A. Oh? What's it all about?
B. Well, to make a long story short, my boss wants me to switch to the night shift, but I'd rather stay on the day shift.
A. Does he feel strongly about your switching to the night shift?
B. Yes, he does. And I feel just as strongly about staying on the day shift.
A. Well, it sounds like a serious disagreement. I hope you can **resolve it**[3] soon.
B. So do I.

I want you to get a haircut.

I'd rather leave my hair long.

1. my mother

I'd like to start a family now.

I'd rather wait until we have a little more money in the bank.

2. my wife

3. my parents

4. my business partner

5. my family

6. my husband

7. the people in my parish

8. my economic advisor

9. some members of my labor union

"A SERIOUS DISAGREEMENT"

Now present your own conversations.

It Doesn't Make Any Difference

(1) have any strong feelings about it
have any feelings about it one way or another
care one way or the other
have a preference/any preferences

(2) It doesn't make any difference (to me).
It doesn't matter (to me).
It's all the same to me.
I don't care.
I don't feel strongly about it one way or the other.

A. When do you want to leave?
B. Oh. I don't know. Whenever you'd like to leave is fine with me.
A. You don't **have any strong feelings about it?**(1)
B. No, not really. **It doesn't make any difference.**(2)

1. Who would you like to invite to the party?

2. What would you like to do this weekend?

3. Which movie would you rather see?

4. How would you like me to cut your hair?

5. Where do you want us to put the couch?

Now present your own conversations.

It's Entirely Up to You

A. **Would you mind**[1] if I went home early?
B. No. I wouldn't mind.
A. Are you sure? I mean if you'd rather I didn't I won't.
B. No. Honestly. It doesn't matter to me whether you go home early or not. **It's entirely up to you.**[2]

[1]   Would you mind
       Would it bother you
       Would it disturb you

[2]   It's (entirely) up to you.
       It's (entirely) your decision.
       It's for you to decide.

1. smoke

2. invite my boss for dinner

3. drop something off at the post office

4. have a date with someone else

5. take away your "security blanket"

Now present your own conversations.

INTERCHANGE
The International Gourmet

A. Welcome to "The International Gourmet." My name is Walter, and I'll be your waiter this evening. Would you like to see the menu, or would you care to order our special complete dinner of the day?

B. What's the special today?

A. Leg of lamb . . . and I highly recommend it.

B. Well . . . Let me see . . . Okay. I think I'll have the special.

A. All right. Now, as an appetizer, you have a choice of fruit salad or tomato juice.

B. Hmm. I think I'd like the fruit salad.

A. All right. And the soups we're offering today are split pea or French onion.

B. Split pea or French onion? Hmm. That's a difficult choice. I guess I'd rather have the split pea.

A. And what kind of dressing would you like on your salad?

B. What do you have?

A. Well, let's see. We have Italian, French, Russian, and blue cheese.

B. I'd prefer Italian.

A. Italian. Fine. Now, with your leg of lamb, you can have your choice of two of our side dishes. Today we're featuring brown rice, baked potato, string beans in a cream sauce, and . . . Hmm . . . Let me see if I can remember them all . . . Oh, yes . . . And we also have fresh squash and marinated mushrooms.

B. That's quite a selection! Let's see . . . uh . . . hmmm. Let me have brown rice and fresh squash.

A. Okay. I think that's it. Oh! I almost forgot. What would you like to drink with your meal?

B. I'll have a glass of red wine.

A. All right. I'll put this order in right away, and I'll be back in a moment with some rolls and butter.

B. Thank you.

A. Welcome to "_____." My name is _____, and I'll be your waiter/waitress this evening. Would you like to see the menu, or would you care to order our special complete dinner of the day?

B. What's the special today?

A. _____ . . . and I highly recommend it.

B. Well . . . Let me see . . . Okay. I think I'll have the special.

A. All right. Now, as an appetizer, you have a choice of _____ or _____.

B. Hmm. I think I'd like the _____.

A. All right. And the soups we're offering today are _____ or _____.

B. _____ or _____? Hmm. That's a difficult choice. I guess I'd rather have the _____.

A. And what kind of dressing would you like on your salad?

B. What do you have?

A. Well, let's see. We have _____, _____, _____, and _____.

B. I'd prefer _____.

A. _____. Fine. Now, with your _____, you can have your choice of two of our side dishes. Today we're featuring _____, _____, _____, and . . . Hmm . . . Let me see if I can remember them all . . . Oh, yes . . . And we also have _____ and _____.

B. That's quite a selection! Let's see . . . uh . . . hmmm. Let me have _____ and _____.

A. Okay. I think that's it. Oh! I almost forgot. What would you like to drink with your meal?

B. I'll have _____.

A. All right. I'll put this order in right away, and I'll be back in a moment with some rolls and butter.

B. Thank you.

You're a waiter or waitress in a restaurant. Give your restaurant a name, design a "special of the day," and then create an original conversation using the model dialog above as a guide. Feel free to adapt and expand the model any way you wish.

(Use the "memo" below to design your "special of the day.")

MEMO TO ALL WAITERS AND WAITRESSES

Please let your customers know that today's special is as follows:

Special of the Day: _____

Appetizers: _____   Soups: _____

_____   _____

Salad Dressings: Side Dishes:

_____ _____   _____ _____

_____ _____   _____ _____

_____

Functions

Preference

Inquiring about . . .

Would you { prefer _____?
rather have _____?
like _____? }

Would you like to
Would you prefer to
Would you rather   } _____ (or
Do you want to   _____)?
Would you care to

How would you like it?

Do you have any strong feelings
about it?
Do you have any feelings about it
one way or another?
Do you care one way or the other?
Do you have a preference/any
preferences?

Expressing . . .

I'd prefer _____.
I'd rather have _____.
I'd like _____.

I'd prefer to _____.
I'd rather _____.
I'd like to _____.
I'd much rather _____.

I'd prefer not to _____.

I feel strongly about _____ing.

If you'd rather I didn't _____ I
won't.

Want-Desire

Inquiring about . . .

When do you want to _____?
Who would you like to _____?
What would you like to do?
How would you like me
to _____?
Which _____ would you rather
_____?
Where do you want _____ to
_____?

Expressing . . .

I'd like _____.
I'll have _____.
I want _____.

I (really) don't feel like _____ing.
I'm not (really) in the mood to
_____.

I'd (really) prefer not to _____.

_____ wants me to _____.

Requests

Direct, More Polite

Would you mind
Would it bother you   } if I _____ed?
Would it disturb you

Indifference

Whenever _____ is fine with me.
(Whoever . . . . Whatever . . . .
However . . . . Whichever . . . .
Wherever . . . .)

It doesn't make any difference (to
me).
It doesn't matter (to me).
It's all the same to me.
I don't care.
I don't feel strongly about it one way
or the other.

It doesn't matter to me whether you
_____ or not.

It's (entirely) up to you.
It's (entirely) your decision.
It's for you to decide.

Conversation Strategy

Hesitating

Well . . .
Let me see . . .
Let's see . . .
Hmm . . .
Okay . . .
Uh . . .
I think . . .
I guess . . .

SCENES & IMPROVISATIONS
Chapters 4, 5, 6

Who do you think these people are?
What do you think they're talking about?
Create conversations based on these scenes and act them out.

1.

2.

3.

4.

5.

6.

7.

8.

Intention
Promising
Invitations
Disappointment

7

Initiating Conversations
Initiating a Topic
Focusing Attention

I Promise
I Won't Let You Down
He Gave Me His Word
I've Made a Decision
I'll Probably Stay Home and Read a Book
I Haven't Made Up My Mind Yet
I Was Planning to Do Room 407 a Little Later
I Changed My Mind

• Embedded Questions • Future: Going to • Future: Will
• Gerunds • Infinitives • Might • Past Continuous
to Express Future Intention • Present Perfect Tense
• Sequence of Tenses • Two-Word Verbs

I Promise

(1) rely on
depend on
count on

(2) I promise I'll
I promise to

A. Can I **rely on**[1] you to turn off the lights when you leave?
B. Yes. **I promise I'll**[2] turn them off.
A. You won't forget? It's really important.
B. Don't worry. You can **rely on**[1] me.

1. pick up the soda for the party tonight

2. bring back my typewriter tomorrow

3. drop off my suit at the cleaner's on the way to school

4. put away your toys before our guests arrive

5. clean up the kitchen before the health inspector gets here

"I PROMISE"

Now present your own conversations.

I Won't Let You Down

A. Will the car be ready by five?
B. Yes, it will.
A. Really? Can I **depend on**(1) that?
B. **Absolutely!**(2) **I promise**(3) it'll be ready by five.
A. Okay. Now remember, I'm **counting**(4) on you.
B. Don't worry! I won't **let you down.**(5)

(1) depend on
    count on
    rely on
    be sure of

(2) Absolutely!
    Definitely!
    Positively!

(3) I promise (you)
    I guarantee (you)
    I assure you
    I give you my word
    You can be sure

(4) counting
    depending
    relying

(5) let you down
    disappoint you

1. Will you write to me often?

2. Will we get to the airport in time for my 3:00 flight?

3. Will there be enough food for all our customers tonight?

4. Will this tooth extraction be painless?

5. Will you behave yourself for the baby-sitter tonight?

Now present your own conversations.

He Gave Me His Word

A. I'm very **disappointed with**(1) the salesman who sold me this watch.
B. How come?
A. He guaranteed me this watch was waterproof, . . . but it isn't!
B. **That's too bad.**(2) Are you going to talk to him about it? After all, he DID give you his word.
A. **Maybe I should.**(3)

A. I'm very **disappointed with**(1) my next-door neighbor.
B. How come?
A. She gave me her word she would keep her dog off my lawn, . . . but she hasn't!
B. **That's a shame.**(2) Are you going to talk to her about it? After all, she DID give you her word.
A. **Maybe I should.**(3)

(1) disappointed with disappointed in	(2) That's too bad. That's/What a shame.	(3) Maybe I should. I guess I will. I suppose I will.

1. my upstairs neighbor

2. my landlord

3. my daughter

4. my boss

5. my employees

6. the photographer

7. my agent in Hollywood

Now present your own conversations.

I've Made a Decision

(1) I'm going to
I'm planning to
I plan to
I intend to
I've decided to

(2) Gee!
Boy!
Wow!

(3) I've thought about it for a
long time
I've given it a lot of thought
I've given it a lot of serious
consideration

A. You know, . . . I've made a decision.
B. What?
A. **I'm going to**[1] join the army.
B. **Gee!**[2] Joining the army! That's a big decision!
A. I know. It is. But **I've thought about it for a long time**[3] and decided it's time to do it.
B. Well, good luck!

1. get married

2. give up smoking

3. sell my house

4. quit my job

5. apply to business school

"I'VE MADE A DECISION"

Now present your own conversations.

I'll Probably Stay Home and Read a Book

A. Hi! It's me!
B. Oh, hi! How are you?
A. Fine. Tell me, what are you doing this afternoon?
B. **I'm not sure.**(1) I'll **probably**(2) stay home and read a book. How about you?
A. Well, I'm planning to go fishing. **Would you like to join me?** (3)
B. Sure. **I'd be happy to.**(4) Going fishing sounds a lot more **exciting**(5) than staying home and reading a book.
A. Good! I'll pick you up at around one o'clock.
B. See you then.

1. work in the garden
   play tennis

2. work on my car
   go swimming

3. do some chores around
   the house
   see the new exhibit at
   the museum

4. work on my term paper
   see a movie

5. catch up on some work at
   the office
   play a few rounds of golf

Now present your own conversations.

I Haven't Made Up My Mind Yet

(1)
I've been thinking of
I'm thinking of
I've been thinking about
I'm thinking about

(2)
I thought I might
I thought I'd
I might
I may

A. Have you decided who you're going to ask to the prom?
B. No. I haven't made up my mind yet. **I've been thinking of**[1] asking Susan, but **I also thought I might**[2] ask Elizabeth.
A. Sounds like a difficult decision. I'll be curious to know what you decide.
B. I'll let you know.
A. Promise?
B. Promise.

1. Chemistry
   Music

2. to Florida
   to Arizona

3. right away
   when business gets better

4. on our next date
   in a long letter

5. an IBM
   an Apple

Now present your own conversations.

I Was Planning to Do Room 407 a Little Later

407

(1) I was planning to
I was going to
I intended to
I thought I would

(2) a little later
in a little while

(3) right away
right now
as soon as I can
the first chance I get

A. Have you done Room 407 yet?
B. No, I haven't. **I was planning to**(1) do it **a little later.**(2)
A. Would you mind doing it soon?
B. No, not at all. I'll do it **right away.**(3)

1. write the monthly report

2. copy my memo

3. distribute the mail

4. make my hotel reservations in Chicago

5. give out the paychecks

Now present your own conversations.

INTERCHANGE
I Changed My Mind

A. Well, if it isn't David Johnson!
B. Richard Peters! It's nice to see you again!
A. You know, David, I've been meaning to call you for a long time.
B. Me, too. How have you been?
A. Fine. How about yourself?
B. Pretty good.
A. Tell me, David. The last time I saw you, you were planning to go to law school, weren't you?
B. Yes, I guess I was. But as it turned out, I changed my mind.
A. Oh, really? But **if I remember correctly,**[1] you were intent on going to law school. Whatever made you change your mind?
B. Well, it's a long story, and I don't want to bore you with all the details. But **what it boils down to is that**[2] I decided that going to law school wasn't a very good idea. I decided to go to medical school instead.
A. Medical school? That's very interesting.
B. And how about you? The last time we talked, didn't you tell me you were going to open your own real estate business?
A. That's right. I was. But things turned out differently.
B. But you seemed so determined to do that. What happened?
A. Well, it's very complicated, and I'm sure you don't want to know all the details. But **as it turned out,**[2] I decided that opening my own real estate company just wasn't for me. So I decided to stay at my old job instead.
B. Well, **a lot sure has happened**[3] since we last saw each other.
A. **I'll say!**[4] You know, we should try to stay in touch.
B. Yes, we should. Let's have lunch together sometime soon.
A. Good idea.
B. Take care now.
A. You, too.

(1) If I remember correctly,
If I recall,
If my memory serves me,

(2) What it boils down to is that
The fact of the matter is that
As it turned out,

(3) a lot (sure) has happened
a lot (sure) has changed
there have been a lot of changes

(4) I'll say!
You can say that again!
You're right.
I agree.

A. Well, if it isn't _____ _____!
B. _____ _____! It's nice to see you again!
A. You know, _____, I've been meaning to call you for a long time.
B. Me, too. How have you been?
A. Fine. How about yourself?
B. Pretty good.
A. Tell me, _____. The last time I saw you, you were planning to _____, weren't you?
B. Yes, I guess I was. But as it turned out, I changed my mind.
A. Oh, really? But **if I remember correctly,**(1) you were intent on _____ing. Whatever made you change your mind?
B. Well, it's a long story, and I don't want to bore you with all the details. But **what it boils down to is that**(2) I decided that _____ing wasn't a very good idea. I decided to _____ instead.
A. _____? That's very interesting.
B. And how about you? The last time we talked, didn't you tell me you were going to _____?
A. That's right. I was. But things turned out differently.
B. But you seemed so determined to do that. What happened?
A. Well, it's very complicated, and I'm sure you don't want to know all the details. But **as it turned out,**(2) I decided that _____ing just wasn't for me. So I decided to _____ instead.
B. Well, **a lot sure has happened**(3) since we last saw each other.
A. **I'll say!**(4) You know, we should try to stay in touch.
B. Yes, we should. Let's have lunch together sometime soon.
A. Good idea.
B. Take care now.
A. You, too.

You've just "bumped into" somebody you haven't seen in a while. Create an original conversation using the model dialog above as a guide. Feel free to adapt and expand the model any way you wish.

Functions

Intention

Inquiring about . . .

Have you decided _____?

What are you doing *this afternoon*?

Expressing . . .

I'm going to _____.
I'm planning to _____.
I plan to _____.
I intend to _____.
I've decided to _____.

I'll _____ {
right away.
right now.
as soon as I can.
the first chance I get.
}

I've been thinking of _____ing.
I'm thinking of _____ing.
I've been thinking about _____ing.
I'm thinking about _____ing.

I've been meaning to _____ (for a long time).

I've thought about it for a long time.
I've given it a lot of thought.
I've given it a lot of serious consideration.

I've decided it's time to do it.

I haven't made up my mind yet.

I was planning to _____.
I was going to _____.
I intended to _____.
I thought I would _____.

I was intent on _____ing.
I was determined to _____.

Promising

Asking for a Promise

Can I {rely on / depend on / count on} you to _____?

Can I {depend on / count on / rely on / be sure of} that?

Promise?

Offering a Promise

Promise.
I promise I'll _____.
I promise to _____.

I promise (you) _____.
I guarantee (you) _____.
I assure you _____.
I give you my word _____.
You can be sure _____.

Absolutely.
Definitely.
Positively.

You can {rely on / depend on / count on} me.

I won't let you down.
I won't disappoint you.

Invitations

Extending . . .

Would you like to join me?
Do you want to join me?
Would you be interested in joining me?

Accepting . . .

I'd be happy to.
I'd love to.
I'd like that.

Disappointment

I'm (very) disappointed with/in _____.

Sympathizing

That's too bad.
That's a/What a shame.

Surprise-Disbelief

Gee!
Boy!
Wow!

Certainty/Uncertainty

Expressing Uncertainty

I'm not sure.
I'm not certain.
I don't know yet.

Probability/Improbability

Expressing Probability

I'll probably _____.
I'll most likely _____.

Possibility/Impossibility

Expressing Possibility

I might _____.
I may _____.
I thought I might _____.
I thought I'd _____.

Agreement/Disagreement

Expressing Agreement

I agree.
You're right.
I'll say.
You can say that again!

Conversation Strategies

Initiating Conversations

Hi! It's me!

Well, if it isn't _____!

Initiating a Topic

You know, . . .

Focusing Attention

What it boils down to is that . . .
The fact of the matter is that . . .
As it turned out, . . .

Offering to Do Something
Offering to Help
Gratitude
Appreciation
Persuading-Insisting

Initiating a Topic

Do You Want Me to Wash the Dishes?
Want Any Help?
Let Me Give You a Hand
May I Help You?
Can I Do Anything to Help?
I'm Very Grateful to You
Words Can't Express . . .

• Can • Demonstrative Adjectives • Gerunds • Indirect
Objects • Passives • Relative Clauses with Who
• Should • Singular/Plural • Want + Object + Infinitive

Do You Want Me to Wash the Dishes?

(1) Do you want me to _____?
Would you like me to _____?
I'll _____, if you'd like.
I'll/I'd be happy/glad to _____, if you'd like.

(2) Don't worry about it.
That's okay/all right.

(3) No, really!
Listen!
(Oh,) come on!

(4) for a change
for once

(5) I appreciate it/that.
I'd appreciate it/that.
It's nice/kind of you to offer.
That's (very) nice/kind of you.
That would be nice.

A. **Do you want me to**[1] wash the dishes?
B. No. **Don't worry about it.**[2] I don't mind washing the dishes.
A. **No, really!**[3] You're always the one who washes the dishes. Let me, **for a change.**[4]
B. Okay. Thanks. **I appreciate it.**[5]

1. water the plants

2. mow the lawn

3. take out the garbage

4. defrost the refrigerator

5. feed the hamster

Now present your own conversations.

Want Any Help?

A. I see you're changing the oil.
B. Yes. It hasn't been changed in a long time.
A. **Want any help?**[1]
B. Sure. **If you don't mind.**[2]
A. No, not at all. **I'd be happy to give you a hand.**[3]
B. Thanks. I appreciate it.

[1] (Do you) want any help?
(Do you) need any help?
(Do you) want a hand?
(Do you) need a hand?
Can I help?
Can I give you a hand?

[2] If you don't mind.
If you wouldn't mind.
If it's no trouble.

[3] I'd be happy/glad to give
you a hand.
I'd be happy/glad to lend a
hand.
I'd be happy/glad to help.

1. clean the garage

2. wash the windows

3. paint the fence

4. sweep out the barn

5. shampoo Rover

"WANT ANY HELP?"

Now present your own
conversations.

Let Me Give You a Hand

(1) Would you like me to help you _____?
Do you want me to help you _____?
I'd be happy/glad to help you _____, (if you'd like).
Let me help you _____.
Would you like any help _____ing?
Would you like me to give you a hand _____ing?

(2) There's no sense in your _____ing
There's no reason (for you) to _____
You don't have to _____
You shouldn't have to _____

(3) it's nice of you to offer
thanks for offering
I appreciate your offering

(4) Look!
Listen!
Come on!

(5) trouble you
bother you
inconvenience you
put you to any trouble
put you out

A. **Would you like me to help you**(1) move that desk?
B. No, that's okay. I can move it myself.
A. Oh, come on! Let me give you a hand. **There's no sense in your**(2) moving it yourself if I'm here to help.
B. Really, **it's nice of you to offer,**(3) but . . .
A. **Look!**(4) I insist! You're not moving that desk by yourself!
B. Well, okay. But I really don't want to **trouble you.**(5)
A. No trouble at all! Honestly! I'm happy to lend a hand.

1. lift that motor

2. carry those boxes

3. take down that sign

4. unload that truck

5. set those chairs up

6. cut that tree down

7. adjust that TV antenna

8. change that tire

9. alphabetize those index cards

Now present your own conversations.

May I Help You?

A. **May I help you?**(1)
B. Not right now, thanks. I'm just looking.
A. **Is there anything in particular I can help you find?**(2)
B. Well, actually, I'm looking for a digital watch.
A. Oh, I'm afraid **we're out of**(3) digital watches, but we expect some in very soon. Is there anything else I can help you with?
B. I guess not. But thanks anyway.
A. Well, **please let me know if I can be of any further assistance.**(4)
B. Thanks very much.

1. a size 40 jacket

2. a convertible sofa-bed

3. size 34 underwear

4. a remote-control video cassette recorder

5. sugar-free chewing gum

Now present your own conversations.

Can I Do Anything to Help?

A. Excuse me. Are you **okay?**[1]
B. Well, uh . . . I'm not sure.
A. What happened?
B. I was knocked down by someone on roller skates.
A. Oh, no! **Can I do anything to help?**[2]
B. **Huh?**[3]
A. Can I help? Should I **call an ambulance?**[4]
B. No, that's okay. I think I'll be all right.
A. Well, here. **Let me**[5] help you up.
B. Thanks. **You're very kind.**[6]
A. **Don't mention it.**[7]

[1] okay
all right

[2] Can I do anything to help?
Is there anything I can do
to help?
Can I help?

[3] Huh?
What?

[4] call/get an ambulance
call/get a doctor
call/get the police

[5] Let me
Allow me to
I'll

[6] You're very kind/nice.
That's (very) kind/nice
of you.

[7] Don't mention it.
You're welcome.
Glad to be of help.
No problem.

1. I was just mugged.

2. I think I sprained my ankle.

3. I was just hit by a car.

4. I fell off my bicycle.

5. I must have fainted.

"CAN I DO ANYTHING TO HELP?"

Now present your own conversations.

I'm Very Grateful to You

A. You know, I keep forgetting to thank you for lending me your calculator.
B. Oh, **it was nothing.**(1)
A. **No, I mean it!**(2) It was very nice of you to lend it to me. **I'm very grateful to you.**(3)
B. **I'm glad I could do it.**(4)

1. loan me your car

2. give me a promotion

3. send me flowers when I was in the hospital

4. create a new position at the company for my daughter

5. fix my son up with your niece

Now present your own conversations.

INTERCHANGE
Words Can't Express . . .

I'm very grateful to receive this award for "Best Actress."
I can't begin to tell you how much I appreciate this honor.
There are many people I'd like to thank.

First of all,[1] I want to thank my parents for bringing me into this world.

I also want to express my gratitude to all of my teachers over the years, but especially to my acting teacher, Vincent Lewis, who taught me everything I know.

And finally, I want to express my appreciation to all of my friends for their **support,**[2] especially to Katherine Miller, for being there when I needed her.

This award means a great deal to me. Words can't express how **honored**[3] I feel at this moment. Thank you very much.

[1] First of all, First and foremost, Most of all, Above all,	[2] support encouragement help advice	assistance guidance inspiration	[3] honored thrilled excited proud overwhelmed

---

I'm very grateful to receive this award for "_____."
I can't begin to tell you how much I appreciate this honor.
There are many people I'd like to thank.

First of all,[1] I want to thank my parents for _____.

I also want to express my gratitude to all of my teachers over the years, but especially to _____, who _____.

And finally, I want to express my appreciation to all of my friends for their _____,[2] especially to _____, for _____.

This award means a great deal to me. Words can't express how _____[3] I feel at this moment. Thank you very much.

You have just received an award. Make your acceptance speech using the model above as a guide. Feel free to adapt and expand the model any way you wish.

Functions

Offering to Do Something

Do you want me to _____?
Would you like me to _____?
I'll _____, if you'd like.
I'll/I'd be happy/glad to _____, if
   you'd like.

Let me (_____).

Offering to Help

Making an Offer

(Do you) want any help?
(Do you) need any help?
(Do you) want a hand?
(Do you) need a hand?
Can I help?
Can I give you a hand?

Would you like me to help you
   _____?
Do you want me to help you
   _____?
I'd be glad/happy to help you
   _____, (if you'd like).
Let me help you _____.
Would you like any help
   _____ing?
Would you like me to give you a
   hand _____ing?

Can I do anything to help?
Is there anything I can do to help?
Can I help?

I'd be happy/glad to give you a
   hand.
I'd be happy/glad to lend a hand.
I'd be happy/glad to help.

Let me give you a hand.
I'm happy to lend a hand.

Let me _____.
Allow me to _____.
I'll _____.

May/Can I help you?
May/Can I assist you?

Is there anything/something in
   particular I can help you find?
Is there anything/something you're
   looking for in particular?

Is there anything else I can help you
   with?

Please let me know if I can be of any
   further assistance.
Please feel free to call on me if I can
   be of any further assistance.
If I can be of any further assistance,
   please don't hesitate to ask/let me
   know.

Responding to an Offer

If you don't mind.
If you wouldn't mind.
If it's no trouble.

I don't want to {
   trouble you.
   bother you.
   inconvenience you.
   put you to any trouble.
   put you out.
}

Don't worry about it.
That's okay/all right.

Gratitude

Expressing . . .

Thanks (very much).
Thank you (very much).

I'm very grateful (to _____).

I want to thank _____.
I want to express my gratitude to
   _____.

I keep forgetting to thank you for
   _____.

Responding to . . .

You're welcome.
Don't mention it.
No problem.
Glad to be of help.
It was nothing (at all).

I'm glad I could do it/help/be of help.
(It was) my pleasure.
Any time.

Appreciation

I appreciate it/that.
I'd appreciate it/that.
It's nice/kind of you to offer.
Thanks for offering.
I appreciate your offering.
That's (very) nice/kind of you.
That would be nice.

You're very kind/nice.

I'm very grateful (to _____).

I really appreciate it.
I appreciate it very much.

It was very nice of you (to
   _____).

I can't begin to tell you how much I
   appreciate _____.

I want to express my appreciation to
   _____.

Persuading-Insisting

Listen!
Look!
(No,) really!
(No,) I mean it!
(No,) honestly!
(Oh,) come on!

I insist.

Let me, for a change.
Let me, for once.

There's no sense in your
   _____ing.
There's no reason (for you) to
   _____.
You don't have to _____.
You shouldn't have to _____.

Attracting Attention

Excuse me.

Conversation Strategy

Initiating a Topic

You know, . . .

Is Smoking Allowed Here?
Please Don't Pick the Flowers
Can I Possibly Have the Car Tonight?
Would You Mind If I Served Leftovers for Dinner?
I'd Rather You Didn't
I Can't Do That Without an Authorization
You Mustn't Under Any Circumstances

• Can/Could • Gerunds • Imperatives • Infinitives • May
• Must • Sequence of Tenses • Short Answers • Would

Is Smoking Allowed Here?

A. **Is** smoking **allowed**[1] here?
B. **Yes, it is.**[2]
A. Thanks.

A. **Are you permitted to** take pictures[1] here?
B. **No, you aren't.**[3]
A. Oh, okay. Thanks.

A. **Are people allowed to** park[1] here?
B. **Yes, they are.**[2]
A. Thanks.

A. **Do they permit** surfing[1] here?
B. **Not as far as I know.**[3]
A. Oh, okay. Thanks.

[1] Is _____ing allowed/ permitted? Is it okay to _____?	[2] Yes, it is. Yes, it is.	[3] No, it isn't. No, it isn't.
Are you allowed/permitted to _____? Are people allowed to _____?	Yes, you are. Yes, they are.	No, you aren't. No, they aren't.
Do they allow/permit _____ing? Do they allow people to _____?	Yes, they do. Yes, they do.	No, they don't. No, they don't.
	[less certain] I think so. I believe so. Yes, as far as I know.	[less certain] I don't think so. I don't believe so. Not as far as I know.

1. swim

2. camp

3. ice skate

4. feed the animals

5. dive

6. picnic

7. play a radio

8. play frisbee

9. sunbathe in the nude

"IS SMOKING ALLOWED HERE?"

Now present your own conversations.

Please Don't Pick the Flowers

A. **Excuse me,**(1) but **I don't think** picking the flowers **is allowed.**(2)
B. Oh?
A. Yes. There's a sign here that says so.
B. Hmm. "Please Don't Pick the Flowers." **How about that!**(3) I never even noticed it. Thanks for telling me.
A. You're welcome.

1.

2.

3.

4.

5.

Now present your own conversations.

Can I Possibly Have the Car Tonight?

Check with your mother.

A. Could I ask you a favor?
B. Sure. What?
A. **Can I possibly**[1] have the car tonight?
B. Hmm. **Let me think for a minute.**[2] Well, **I guess so.**[3] But maybe you should also check with your mother. I'm sure she won't **object to**[4] your having the car tonight, but it wouldn't hurt to ask.
A. Okay. Thanks. I'll check with her right away.

[1] Can/Could I (possibly)
  _____?
  Can/Could I please _____?
  May I (please) _____?
  Is it all right/okay (with you)
    if I _____?
  Would it be possible for me
    to _____?
  I'd like to _____, if that's
    all right/okay (with you).

[2] Let me think (for a
    minute).
  Let me see.
  Let's see now.

[3] I guess so.
  I suppose so.
  I don't see (any reason)
    why not.

[4] object to
  have any objection to
  mind

Check with Mrs. Fleming.

1. go home an hour early
today

Check with your father.

2. stay over at Lucy's house
tonight

Check with my roommate.

3. borrow your TV until
tomorrow

Check with our
manager, Mr. Larson.

4. stay in my room a few hours
past check-out time

Check with the owners
of the building.

5. put a hot tub on my
balcony

"CAN I POSSIBLY
HAVE THE
CAR TONIGHT?"

Now present your own
conversations.

Would You Mind If I Served Leftovers for Dinner?

A. **Would you mind if I** served leftovers for dinner?[1]
B. **No, I wouldn't mind.**[2]
A. Are you sure? I mean if you'd rather I didn't I won't.
B. **Honestly.**[3] If you want to serve leftovers for dinner, it's **fine**[4] with me. **Go right ahead.**[5]

A. **Is it all right with you if I** turn up the heat?[1]
B. **Certainly.**[2]
A. Are you sure? I mean if you'd rather I didn't I won't.
B. **Honestly.**[3] If you want to turn up the heat, it's **fine**[4] with me. **Go right ahead.**[5]

---

[1] Would you mind/object if I _____ed? Would it bother you if I _____ed? Do you mind if I _____? $\longrightarrow$	[2] No, I wouldn't mind. No, I don't mind. No, of course not. No, not at all. No, it's all right/fine/okay with me. No.
Is it all right/okay (with you) if I _____? Would it be all right/okay (with you) if I _____ed? I'd like to _____, if that's all right/okay (with you). $\longrightarrow$	Certainly. Sure. Of course. By all means. It's all right/okay with me. Yes.

- -

[3] Honestly. Really.	[4] fine all right okay	[5] Go (right) ahead. Be my guest.

1. Would you mind . . .?

2. Is it all right you with you . . .?

3. Would it bother you . . .?

4. I'd like to . . .

5. Do you mind . . .?

6. Would you object . . .?

7. Would it be all right with you . . .?

8. Is it okay with you . . .?

9. Would it bother you . . .?

Now present your own conversations.

89

I'd Rather You Didn't

A. Is it all right if I order steak for two?
B. **Actually,**[1] **I'd rather you didn't.**[2]
A. Oh, okay.
B. **You see**[3] . . . I'm a vegetarian.
A. Oh, I'm sorry. I didn't know that.

1. Would you mind . . .?

2. Do you mind . . .?

3. Would it be okay . . .?

4. Would you object . . .?

5. Is it okay . . .?

Now present your own conversations.

I Can't Do That Without an Authorization

the landlord

A. Could I ask you to change the lock on our door?
B. I'm afraid I can't do that without **an authorization from**[1] the landlord.
A. Oh? How can I get his authorization?
B. Well, the best thing to do is to write a note asking him to **authorize me to**[2] change the lock on your door.
A. Okay. I'll do that.
B. I'm sorry. I don't mean to **make things difficult for you.**[3]
A. I understand.

[1] an authorization from
the permission of
the approval of
the consent of
the agreement of
a go ahead from

[2] authorize me to _____
permit me to _____
approve my _____ing
consent to my _____ing
agree to my _____ing
give the go ahead for me
   to _____

[3] make things difficult/
   complicated for you
complicate things
give you a hard time
give you "the runaround"

Mrs. Field in the Maintenance Department

1. fix the ceiling in my office

Mr. Thompson in the Payroll Department

2. give me an advance on my next paycheck

Mr. Blackwell in the Dean's office

3. switch my major to Accounting

the branch manager, Mrs. Watkins

4. hold our mail at the post office while we're away

the board of directors

5. change my title to "Senior Vice-President"

"I CAN'T DO THAT WITHOUT AN AUTHORIZATION"

Now present your own conversations.

INTERCHANGE
You Mustn't Under Any Circumstances

A. Before you sign the lease, do you have any questions?
B. Yes. Are we allowed to sublet the apartment?
A. No. I'm afraid subletting the apartment isn't permitted.
B. I see. Well, is it all right to use the fireplace?
A. No. You mustn't use the fireplace under any circumstances.
B. Oh. Well, do you allow people to have pets?
A. No. That's out of the question. We don't permit anyone to have pets.
B. How about parking in front of the building?
A. I'm sorry. You're not supposed to park in front of the building.
B. Oh.
A. And before I forget, I should mention that you may not alter the apartment in any way without permission. Now, do you have any other questions?
B. No, I guess not. I think you've answered them all.

A. Before _____, do you have any questions?
B. Yes. Are we allowed to _____?
A. No. I'm afraid _____ing isn't permitted.
B. I see. Well, is it all right to _____?
A. No. You mustn't _____ under any circumstances.
B. Oh. Well, do you allow people to _____?
A. No. That's out of the question. We don't permit anyone to _____.
B. How about _____ing?
A. I'm sorry. You're not supposed to _____.
B. Oh.
A. And before I forget, I should mention that you may not _____ without permission. Now, do you have any other questions?
B. No, I guess not. I think you've answered them all.

1. Before you begin your freshman year here at Winchester College . . .

2. Before beginning your summer here at Camp Salamander . . .

3. Before you start your six weeks of basic training . . .

4. Before your tour of The Republic of Grenomia gets underway . . .

Create original conversations using the model dialog on p. 92 as a guide. Feel free to adapt and expand the model any way you wish.

Functions

Permission

Asking for . . .

Can/Could I (possibly) _____?
Can/Could I please _____?
May I (please) _____?
Is it all right/okay (with you) if I
_____?
Would it be possible for me to
_____?
I'd like to _____, if that's all
right/okay (with you).

Would you mind/object if I
_____ed?
Would it bother you if I
_____ed?
Do you mind if I _____?

Is it all right/okay (with you) if I
_____?
Would it be all right/okay (with you)
if I _____ed?
I'd like to _____, if that's all
right/okay (with you).

Granting . . .

Certainly.
Sure.
Of course.
By all means.
It's all right/okay with me.
Yes.

No, I wouldn't mind.
No, I don't mind.
No, of course not.
No, not at all.
No, it's all right/fine/okay with me.
No.

Go (right) ahead.
Be my guest.

I guess so.
I suppose so.
I don't see (any reason) why not.

If you want to _____,
it's {fine / all right / okay} with me.

Denying . . .

I'd rather you didn't.
I'd prefer it if you didn't/wouldn't.
I'd prefer/rather that you not.
I'd prefer you not to.

_____ing isn't allowed/permitted.
You mustn't _____ (under any
circumstances).
We don't permit anyone to _____.
You're not supposed to _____.
You may not _____ (without
permission).

That's out of the question.

I can't do that without
{an authorization from / the permission of / the approval of / the consent of / the agreement of / a go ahead from} _____.

Inquiring about Permissibility

Is _____ing allowed/permitted?
Is it okay to _____?
Is it all right to _____?
Are you allowed/permitted to _____?
Are people allowed to _____?
Do they allow/permit _____ing?
Do they allow people to _____?

Indicating Permissibility

I don't think _____ing is
allowed/permitted.
I don't think you're allowed/
permitted to _____.
I don't think people are allowed/
permitted to _____.
I don't think they allow/permit
people to _____.
I don't think they allow/permit you
to _____.

Yes, _____ _____.
[less certain]
I think so.
I believe so.
Yes, as far as I know.

No, _____ _____.
[less certain]
I don't think so.
I don't believe so.
Not as far as I know.

Gratitude

Expressing . . .

Thanks (for telling me).

Apologizing

(Oh,) I'm sorry.

I don't mean to
{make things difficult/ complicated for you. / complicate things. / give you a hard time. / give you "the runaround."}

Attracting Attention

Excuse me, . . .
Pardon me, . . .

Surprise-Disbelief

Oh?

(Well,) how about that!
(Well,) what do you know!
(Well,) how do you like that!
Isn't that something!

Persuading-Insisting

Honestly.
Really.

Denying/Admitting

Admitting

You see . . .
The reason is . . .

Requests

Direct, Polite

Could I ask you to _____?

Could I ask you a favor?

Conversation Strategy

Hesitating

Hmm.

Let me think (for a minute).
Let me see.
Let's see now.

SCENES & IMPROVISATIONS
Chapters 7, 8, 9

Who do you think these people are?
What do you think they're talking about?
Create conversations based on these scenes and act them out.

1.

2.

3.

4.

5.

6.

7.

8.

INVENTORY OF FUNCTIONS AND CONVERSATION STRATEGIES

Functions

Advice-Suggestions

Asking for . . .

Any suggestions? 5

Offering . . .

You should _____.
Why don't you _____?
How about _____ing? 3

Why don't you _____? 5

How about _____ing?
What about _____ing?
Let's _____.
Why don't we _____?
We could _____.
Would you be interested in _____(ing)? 5

Maybe we should _____.
Maybe we shouldn't _____. 5

They say that _____ is very good.
One of my favorite _____s is _____. 5

Is _____ okay? 5

Agreement/Disagreement

Expressing Agreement

I agree (with you).
You're right.
[less formal]
I'll say!
You can say that again! 7

Apologizing

I'm sorry.
Excuse me. 1

(Oh,) I'm sorry. 9

I don't mean to { make things difficult/complicated for you. complicate things. give you a hard time. give you "the runaround." 9

Appreciation

I appreciate it/that.
I'd appreciate it/that.
It's nice/kind of you to offer.
Thanks for offering.
I appreciate your offering.
That's (very) nice/kind of you.
That would be nice. 8

I really appreciate it.
I appreciate it very much. 8

It was very nice of you (to _____). 8

I want to express my appreciation to _____. 8

I can't begin to tell you how much I appreciate _____. 8

You're very kind/nice. 8

Asking for and Reporting Information

Where are you from?
  Japan.
What do you do?
  I'm an English teacher.
Which *apartment do you live in?*
How long *have you been studying here?*
Who *is your doctor?*
Whose *family are you in?*
What kind of *music do you play?*
When *are you due?* 1

How about you?
What about you?
And you? 1

Have you { heard from run into talked to seen spoken to been in touch with } _____ lately? 2

How's _____ doing?
How is _____?
How has _____ been? 2
  Fine.
  Great.
  Wonderful.
  Not too well.
  Not so well.
  Not very well 2

Did _____ have anything to say? 1

Have you heard anything about _____?
Do you know anything about _____? 2

Tell me a little about yourself. 2

What do you want to know?
What would you like to know?
What can I tell you? 2

Do you/Would you (by any chance) know _____?
Do you/Would you (by any chance) happen to know _____? 3

Could you (please/possibly)tell me _____?
Do you/Would you (by any chance) know _____?
Can you (please) tell me _____?
Would you (possibly/by any chance) be able to tell me _____? 4

Did you hear (that) _____? 3

Where did you hear that?
How do you know (that)?
Who told you (that)? 3

School isn't really going to be closed tomorrow, is it? 3

What happened? 3

Have you by any chance ever _____ed? 3

Can you tell me what it's like? 3

Which one is that? 3

People say . . .
They say . . .
People/They tell me . . .
Everybody says . . .
Everybody tells me . . .
I've heard . . .
Word has it (that) . . . 2

I heard it on the radio/on TV/on the news.
I saw/read it in the paper. 3

Asking for and Reporting Additional Information

What else have you heard?
Have you heard anything else?
Do you know anything else? 2

Can you tell me anything else?
Can you tell me anything more?
What else can you tell me? 3

What did you do next?
What did you do after that?
And then what did you do?
What was the next thing you did? 3

What else would you like to know? 3

As a matter of fact, . . .
In fact, . . . 3

Attracting Attention

Excuse me, . . .
Pardon me, . . . 8,9

Certainty/Uncertainty

Inquiring about . . .

Are you positive/certain/sure (about that)? 3

Expressing Certainty

I'm positive/certain/sure.
I'm absolutely positive/certain/sure.
I'm a hundred percent sure.
There's no doubt about it.
I'm absolutely positive. 3

Expressing Uncertainty

I don't know for sure.
I'm not (completely/absolutely) positive.
I'm not a hundred percent positive. 3

I'm not sure.
I'm not certain.
I don't know yet. 9

I don't think so.
Not as far as I know. 3

I doubt it. 3

Complaining

It's too _____. 5

I was (a little) disappointed.
I wasn't very pleased with it.
It was (a little) disappointing. 5

I'm { annoyed with / upset with / [stronger] / mad at / angry at / furious with } _____. 5

He's always / He's constantly / He keeps on } _____ing. 5

His _____ing { bothers / annoys / upsets } me. 5

I'm tired of _____(ing).
I'm sick of _____(ing).
I'm sick and tired of _____(ing). 5

Complimenting

Expressing Compliments

That was { a very good / quite a / [less formal] / some } _____! 5

I thought it was { excellent. / wonderful. / terrific. / magnificent. / fabulous. / superb. } 5

I (really) like _____.
I love _____. 5

It's very _____.
It's so _____. 5

It's one of the _____est _____s I've ever _____ed. 5

Responding to Compliments

Thanks/Thank you (for saying so).
It's nice of you to say so/that.
I'm glad you like it. 5

Oh/Aw, go on!
Oh/Aw, come on!
Oh! 5

You're just saying that. 5

A-2

Congratulating

That's fantastic!
That's great/wonderful/exciting/marvelous! 2

Congratulations! 2

I'm very happy to hear that.
I'm very happy for you. 2

Deduction

You must be _____. 2

Denying/Admitting

Admitting

You see . . .
The reason is . . . 9

Describing

He's/She's about your height, sort of *heavy*, with *dark curly* hair. 2

He's/She's very _____. 2

It's the _____one with the _____. 3

It's a (very) _____ _____. 3

It's one of the _____est _____s I know. 3

Directions-Location

Asking for Directions

Could you please tell me how to get to _____? 4

Giving Directions

Go to _____.
Turn _____.
Walk _____ blocks. 4

Disappointment

I was (a little) disappointed.
I wasn't very pleased with it.
It was (a little) disappointing. 5

I'm (very) disappointed with/in _____. 7

Gratitude

Expressing . . .

Thanks (very much).
Thank you (very much). 8

Thanks (for telling me). 9

Thank you for *saying so*.
It's nice of you to *say that/so*. 5

I'm very grateful (to _____). 8

I want to thank _____.
I want to express my gratitude to _____. 8

I keep forgetting to thank you for _____. 8

Responding to . . .

You're welcome.
Don't mention it.
No problem.
Glad to be of help.
It was nothing (at all). 8

I'm glad I could do it/help/be of help.
(It was) my pleasure.
Any time. 8

Greeting People

Hello.
[less formal]
Hi.
[more formal]
How do you do? 1

(It's) nice to meet you.
(It's) nice meeting you.
(I'm) happy to meet you.
(I'm) glad to meet you.
(I'm) pleased to meet you. 1

How are you?
How have you been?
[less formal]
How are you doing?
How are things?
How's it going?
  Fine (thank you/thanks).
  Good.
  All right.
  Okay.
  Not bad. 1

Identifying

My friend *Paul*, my brother *Tom*, . . .

She's the one who _____. 1

The one *the children gave you*. 3

Indifference

Whenever _____ is fine with me.
(Whoever . . . Whatever . . . However . . . Whichever . . . Wherever. . .) 6

It doesn't make any difference (to me).
It doesn't matter (to me).
It's all the same to me.
I don't care
I don't feel strongly about it one way or the other. 6

It doesn't matter to me whether you _____ or not. 6

It's (entirely) up to you.
It's (entirely) your decision.
It's for you to decide. 6

Instructing

(Please) _____. 4

First, . . .
Then, . . .
After that, . . .
Next, . . .
And finally, . . . 4

Intention

Inquiring about . . .

What are you doing *this afternoon?* 7

Have you decided _____? 7

Expressing . . .

I'm going to _____.
I'm planning to _____.
I plan to _____.
I intend to _____.
I've decided to _____. 7

I've been thinking of _____ing.
I'm thinking of _____ing.
I've been thinking about _____ing.
I'm thinking about _____ing. 7

I've been meaning to _____ (for a long time). 7

I've thought about it for a long time.
I've given it a lot of thought.
I've given it a lot of serious consideration. 7

I've decided it's time to do it. 7

I haven't made up my mind yet. 7

I was planning to _____.
I was going to _____.
I intended to _____.
I thought I would _____. 7

I was intent on _____ing.
I was determined to _____. 7

I'll _____ { right away. / right now. / as soon as I can. / the first chance I get. 7

Introductions

Introducing Oneself

My name is _____.
I'm _____. 1

Introducing Others

Let me introduce (you to) _____.
I'd like to introduce (you to) _____.
I'd like you to meet _____.
[less formal]
Meet _____.
This is _____. 1

Invitations

Extending . . .

Would you like to join me?
Do you want to join me?
Would you be interested in joining me? 7

Accepting . . .

I'd love to.
I'd like to.
I'd like that. 7

Likes/Dislikes

Inquiring about . . .

How do you like _____?
What do you think of _____? 5

How did you like _____? 5

Did you like _____? 5

Don't you like _____? 5

Expressing Likes

I like _____.
I love _____. 5

Expressing Dislikes

I don't (really) like/enjoy _____ very much.
I don't (particularly) care for _____.
I'm not (really) crazy about _____.
[stronger]
I hate _____. 5

Offering to Do Something

Do you want me to _____?
Would you like me to _____?
I'll _____, if you'd like.
I'll/I'd be happy/glad to _____, (if you'd like). 8

Let me (_____). 8

Offering to Help

Making an Offer

(Do you) want any help?
(Do you) need any help?
(Do you) want a hand?
(Do you) need a hand?
Can I help?
Can I give you a hand? 8

Would you like me to help you _____?
Do you want me to help you _____?
I'd be glad/happy to help you _____, (if you'd like).
Let me help you _____.
Would you like any help _____ing?
Would you like me to give you a hand _____ing? 8

Can I do anything to help?
Is there anything I can do to help?
Can I help? 8

I'd be happy/glad to give you a hand.
I'd be happy/glad to lend a hand.
I'd be happy/glad to help. 8

Let me give you a hand.
I'm happy to lend a hand. 8

Let me _____.
Allow me to _____.
I'll _____. 8

May/Can I help you?
May/Can I assist you? 8

Is there anything/something in particular I can help you find?
Is there anything/something you're looking for in particular? 8

Is there anything else I can help you with? 8

Please let me know if I can be of any further assistance.
Please feel free to call on me if I can be of any further assistance.
If I can be of any further assistance, please don't hesitate to ask/let me know. 8

Responding to an Offer

If you don't mind.
If you wouldn't mind.
If it's no trouble. 8

I don't want to { trouble you. / bother you. / inconvenience you. / put you to any trouble. / put you out. 8

Don't worry about it.
That's okay/all right. 8

Permission

Asking for . . .

Can/Could I (possibly) _____?
Can/Could I please _____?
May I (please) _____?
Is it all right/okay (with you) if I _____?
Would it be possible for me to _____?
I'd like to _____, if that's all right/okay (with you). 9
Would it be all right/okay (with you) if I _____ed? 9

Would you mind/object if I _____ed?
Would it bother you if I _____ed?
Do you mind if I _____?

Granting . . .

Certainly.
Sure.
Of course.
By all means.
It's all right/okay with me.
Yes. 9

No, I wouldn't mind.
No, I don't mind.
No, of course not.
No, not at all.
No, it's all right/fine/okay with me.
No. 9

Go (right) ahead.
Be my guest. 9

I guess so.
I suppose so.
I don't see (any reason) why not. 9

If you want to _____, it's { fine / all right / okay } with me. 9

Denying . . .

I'd rather you didn't.
I'd prefer it if you didn't/wouldn't.
I'd prefer/rather that you not.
I'd prefer you not to. 9

A-3

_____ing isn't allowed/permitted.
You mustn't _____(under any circumstances).
We don't permit anyone to _____.
You're not supposed to _____.
You may not _____ (without permission).   9

That's out of the question.   9

I can't do that without
$\left\{\begin{array}{l}\text{an authorization from} \\ \text{the permission of} \\ \text{the approval of} \\ \text{the consent of} \\ \text{the agreement of} \\ \text{a go ahead from}\end{array}\right\}$ _____.   9

Inquiring about Permissibility

Is _____ing allowed/permitted?
Is it okay to _____?
Is it all right to _____?
Are you allowed/permitted to _____?
Are people allowed to _____?
Do they allow/permit _____ing?
Do they allow people to _____?   9

Indicating Permissibility

I don't think _____ing is allowed/permitted.
I don't think you're allowed/permitted to _____.
I don't think people are allowed/ permitted to _____.
I don't think they allow/permit people to _____.
I don't think they allow/permit you to _____.   9

Yes, _____ _____.
[less certain]
I think so.
I believe so.
Yes, as far as I know.   9

No, _____ _____.
[less certain]
I don't think so.
I don't believe so.
Not as far as I know.   9

Persuading-Insisting

I mean it!
I'm (really) serious.
I'm being honest with you.   5

Listen!
Look!
(No,) really!
(No,) I mean it!
(No,) honestly!
(Oh,) come on!   8,9

I insist.   8

Let me, for a change.
Let me, for once.   8

There's no sense in your _____ing.
There's no reason (for you) to _____.
You don't have to _____.
You shouldn't have to _____.   8

Possibility/Impossibility

Expressing Possibility

I might _____.
I may _____.
I thought I might _____.
I thought I'd _____.   7

Preference

Inquiring about . . .

Would you $\left\{\begin{array}{l}\text{prefer} \_\_\_\_\_? \\ \text{rather have} \_\_\_\_\_? \\ \text{like} \_\_\_\_\_?\end{array}\right.$ 6

Would you like to
Would you prefer to
Would you rather $\Big\}$ ___ (or ___)?
Do you want to
Would you care to   6

How would you like it?   6

Do you have any strong feelings about it?
Do you have any feelings about it one way or another?
Do you care one way or the other?
Do you have a preference/any preferences?   6

Expressing . . .

I'd prefer _____.
I'd rather have _____.
I'd like _____.

I'd prefer to _____.
I'd rather _____.
I'd like to _____.
I'd much rather _____.   6

I'd prefer not to _____.   6

I feel strongly about _____ing.   6

If you'd rather I didn't _____ I won't.   6

Probability/Improbability

Expressing Probability

I'll probably _____.
I'll most likely _____.   7

Promising

Asking for a Promise

Can I $\left\{\begin{array}{l}\text{rely on} \\ \text{depend on} \\ \text{count on}\end{array}\right\}$ you to _____?   7

Can I $\left\{\begin{array}{l}\text{depend on} \\ \text{count on} \\ \text{rely on} \\ \text{be sure of}\end{array}\right\}$ that?   7

Promise?   7

Offering a Promise

Promise.
I promise I'll _____.
I promise to _____.   7

I promise (you) _____.
I guarantee (you) _____.
I assure you _____.
I give you my word _____.
You can be sure _____.   7

Absolutely.
Definitely.
Positively.   7

You can $\left\{\begin{array}{l}\text{rely on} \\ \text{depend on} \\ \text{count on}\end{array}\right\}$ me.   7

I won't let you down.
I won't disappoint you.   7

Remembering/Forgetting

Inquiring about . . .

Did you (happen to) remember to _____?
You didn't (by any chance) remember to _____, did you?   3

Indicating . . .

You remember.   3

Oh, that one.   3

I forgot (all about it).
I completely forgot.
It (completely) slipped my mind.   3

Requests

Direct, Polite

Could I ask you a favor?
Could I ask you to _____?   9

Direct, More Polite

Could you possibly _____?
Could you (please) _____?
Could I (possibly) ask you to _____?
Would you be willing to _____?   2

Would you mind
Would it bother you $\Big\}$ if I _____ed?
Would it disturb you   6

Satisfaction/Dissatisfaction

Inquiring about . . .

How do you like _____?
What do you think of _____?   5

How did you like _____?   5

Did you (really) like it?   5

Are you $\left\{\begin{array}{l}\text{satisfied} \\ \text{happy} \\ \text{pleased}\end{array}\right\}$ with it?   5

Is it _____ enough?   5

What seems to be the problem (with it)?
What seems to be the matter (with it)?
What's the problem/the matter/wrong (with it)?   5

Expressing Satisfaction

It's $\begin{cases} \text{fine.} \\ \text{very nice.} \\ \text{perfect.} \end{cases}$ 5

It's just what I $\begin{cases} \text{had in mind.} \\ \text{wanted.} \\ \text{was looking for.} \end{cases}$ 5

I wouldn't want it any _____er.   5

Expressing Dissatisfaction

It's too _____.   5

I really $\begin{cases} \text{expected it to be} \\ \text{thought it would be} \\ \text{hoped it would be} \end{cases}$ _____er.   5

It wasn't as _____ as I thought it would be.   5

Surprise-Disbelief

Assistant manager?!
They're going to make the park across the street into a parking lot?!   2,3

School isn't really going to be closed tomorrow, is it?   3

Oh?   9

You're kidding!
No kidding!
You're joking!
I don't/can't believe it.
Oh, come on!
No!
That can't be!
You've got to be kidding!   3

Gee!
Boy!
Wow!   7

(Well,) how about that!
(Well,) what do you know!
(Well,) how do you like that!
Isn't that something!   9

Sympathizing

That's too bad!
That's a shame/a pity!
What a shame/a pity!   2,7

I'm (very) sorry to hear (about) that.
I'm (very/so) sorry.   2

Want-Desire

Inquiring about . . .

When do you want to _____?
Who would you like to _____?
What would you like to do?
How would you like me to _____?
Which _____ would you rather _____?
Where do you want _____ to _____?   6

Expressing . . .

I'd like _____.
I'll have _____.
I want _____.   6

I (really) don't feel like _____ing.
I'm not (really) in the mood to _____.
I don't think I'm in the mood to _____.

I'd (really) prefer not to _____.   6

_____ wants me to _____.   6

Conversation Strategies

Asking for Repetition

(Sorry.) I didn't hear you.   4

I didn't (quite) catch that.
I didn't get that.
I missed that.
I'm lost.
I'm not following you.   4

What did you say?
Could/Would you (please) repeat that?
Could/Would you say that again?
Would you mind saying that again?
Would you mind repeating that?   4

WHEN do you want me to _____?
WHEN should I _____?
WHEN did you tell me to _____?   4

Could you repeat the last two $\begin{cases} \text{instructions?} \\ \text{directions?} \\ \text{steps?} \\ \text{things you said?} \end{cases}$ 4

I forgot the last part.   4

Checking and Indicating Understanding

Checking Another Person's Understanding

(Have you) got it?
Do you follow me?
Okay?   4

Are you with me (so far)?
Okay (so far)?
Are you following me (so far)?   4

Do you think you've got it now?
Have you got all that?   4

Checking One's Own Understanding

Let me see.
Let me see if I understand.
Let me see if I've got that (right).
Let me repeat that back.   4

Indicating Understanding

Now I've got it.
I understand.
I see.
I'm with you.   4

Uh-húh.
Um-hḿm.
Yes.
(That's) right.   4

Focusing Attention

As a matter of fact, . . .
In fact, . . .   3

If you ask me, . . .
In my opinion, . . .
As far as I'm concerned, . . .   3

What it boils down to is that . . .
The fact of the matter is that . . .
As it turned out, . . .   7

Hesitating

Hmm.   6,9

Uh . . .   6

Gee-uh . . .   2

Well . . .   6

Let me see . . .
Let's see . . .
(Well,) let's see . . .
Let's see now . . .   2,6,9

Let me think (for a minute).   9

I think . . .
I guess . . .   6

I don't know where to begin.
I don't know where to start.
I don't know what to say.   2

Initiating Conversations

Excuse me, but . . .
Pardon me, but . . .   1

I don't think we've met.   1

Don't I know you from somewhere?   1

Hi! It's me!   7

Well, if it isn't _____!   7

Initiating a Topic

You know, . . .   7,8

I have some good/bad news.   2

Have you heard the news?   3

Guess _____!
You won't believe _____!   18

CHAPTER 1

Pages 2–3: "I Don't Think We've Met"

Model

- In the United States it is common to initiate a conversation by introducing oneself.
- "Hello." is both formal and informal. "Hi." is informal, and therefore a more common form of greeting. "How do you do?" is a formal greeting.
- The subject and verb are often omitted in conversation as in "(It's) nice to meet you." and "(I'm) happy to meet you."
- Appropriate questions to ask when people meet for the first time often involve what the two speakers have in common. For example, in an English class: "Where are you from?"; at a clinic: "Who is your doctor?"
- "What do you do?" is a very common question asked when two people meet. In the United States, profession and personal identity are very strongly linked.
- It is NOT appropriate for people meeting for the first time to ask about salary, age, marital status, or religion.
- Short answers to information questions are more common in conversation than full-sentence answers. For example, "Where are you from?" "Japan.", as opposed to "I'm from Japan." ("What do you do?" requires a full answer: "I'm a dancer.")

Exercises

6: "Major"—the field or major course of study (such as History, Chemistry, Philosophy) chosen by college students.

Page 4: "Let Me Introduce . . ."

Model

- The greetings "How are you doing?", "How are things?", and "How's it going?" are informal. "How are you?" and "How have you been?" are used in both formal and informal situations.
- "Meet_____." and "This is _____." are lines of introduction that are used in very informal situations.
- Short answers such as "Fine." and "All right." are very common in both formal and informal situations.
- The exchange: "How are you?" "Fine." has become almost a ritual in American society. The speaker asking the question "How are you?" is not necessarily asking how the other person is feeling, but rather is extending a greeting. In response to this "greeting," the other speaker automatically answers "Fine.", "Good." even if he or she isn't!

Page 5: "Don't I Know You From Somewhere?"

Model

- "Excuse me, but . . ." is a common way to initiate a conversation. In this case, it is said with hesitation because Speaker A is not absolutely sure who Speaker B is.
- When a speaker uses a negative question to get information, the speaker expects a positive answer.
- The question "Don't I know you from somewhere?" is so common that it has become a type of cliché. It is sometimes used to indicate that the speaker has an ulterior motive (usually in striking up a conversation with a member of the opposite sex).
- In line 3, Speaker A is positive that he is correct and persists by saying "Sure." or "Of course."
- In line 4, Speaker B realizes that Speaker A has made a mistake. "No, I'm afraid not." and "You must have me confused with somebody else." are very polite ways of telling Speaker A that he is wrong.

Exercises

2: In the United States, boys and girls often play on the same team in certain sports such as baseball and tennis.
5: The FBI (Federal Bureau of Investigation) is the U.S. government agency that investigates federal crimes.
5: The "10 Most Wanted" list is a constantly updated list of the most dangerous and sought-after criminals in the country.

Pages 6–7: "Guess Who I Saw Yesterday!"

Models

- To say "Guess . . ." and "You won't believe . . ." are powerful ways to initiate a new topic of conversation and to capture the interest of the listener. These phrases signal to the listener that the topic and related information will be interesting and relevant.
- In line 6, the phrase "Oh, sure you do!" emphasizes that Speaker A is VERY sure that Speaker B knows the person being talked about.
- In line 10, by saying "How IS she?", Speaker B is enthusiastically asking for information about the person mentioned.

Exercises

5: "Board of Education." Each city in the United States has a board or committee which makes major decisions concerning schools in the area.
6: "Have a crush on"—be infatuated with a member of the opposite sex.
7: "Retirement." When many older Americans stop working, usually around the age of 65, they often move to a warmer climate to spend their retirement years.

CHAPTER 2

Page 10: "Good News!"

Model

- "I have some good news." is a common way to get someone's attention and set the scene for a happy announcement.
- In line 2, Speaker B is expressing interest in Speaker A's good news by saying "Really?"
- In lines 4, 5, and 7, Speaker B appropriately reacts to Speaker A's good news by congratulating her friend.

Exercises

1: "A raise"—a raise in pay or salary.
2: Oxford University is an extremely prestigious British university. For an American to be accepted by Oxford is a great honor.
3: Nobel Prizes are awarded annually to people who work for the interests of humanity. Examples are the Nobel Peace Prize, the Nobel Prize for Medicine, and the Nobel Prize for Literature.
4: Many companies in the United States give awards and recognition to hardworking employees as an incentive.

Page 11: "Bad News!"

Model

- "I have some bad news." prepares the listener for an unpleasant announcement. The listener hears this and is prepared to sympathize.

Exercises

1: In the United States, dogs and cats are usually considered "members of the family." For most Americans, losing a pet is a very serious matter.

Pages 12–13: "Have You Heard from . . . ?"

Models

- To "hear from" and "be in touch with" can mean by letter or by telephone. To "talk to" and "speak to" can mean by telephone or face to face. To "run into" and "see" mean to meet someone face to face.
- In line 3, Speaker B says "As a matter of fact, I have." because it is a coincidence that Speaker A has mentioned that person.
- Even though the subject of the conversation is not present, it is appropriate to express congratulations or sympathy about what has been reported.

Exercises

6: The PTA (Parent Teacher Association) is a group of parents whose children attend the same school and who often meet with the school's teachers and other parents to discuss school issues.

Page 14: "What Do They Look Like?"

Model

- In line 3, Speaker B says, "I'm afraid I don't remember what he looks like." as a polite way of asking Speaker A to describe the person.
- In line 5, Speaker A uses the expression, "You can't miss him." meaning that Charlie Jones is VERY recognizable.
- When describing someone, the adjectives "heavy" and "thin" are more appropriate and polite than the adjectives "fat" and "skinny," which can be insulting.

Exercises

3: "Ms." is a title for women which is commonly used in the United States in place of both Miss and Mrs.

Page 15: "What Are They Like?"

Model

- In the expressions "They say . . ." and "They tell me . . . ," the pronoun "they" is used to mean "everybody" or "many people."
- In line 4, by saying "Hmm.", Speaker A is acknowledging the new information he has heard.
- In line 6, the phrase "Really? That's interesting." has very little meaning. It is most often used simply to acknowledge that the new information has been heard and understood.

Exercises

4: A senator is a U.S. political representative. Two senators from each of the fifty states are elected to represent their state in the United States Senate in Washington, D.C.

Pages 16–17: "Tell Me a Little About Yourself"

Model

- In the first line, "So" signals a change in the topic of conversation.
- "Gee—uh . . ." and "Well, let's see . . ." are common ways to hesitate and give oneself time to think before speaking.
- "Tell me a little about yourself." is a very open-ended request. It is a common way of asking for information about a person being met for the first time.

- "What do you do?" (line 4) is probably the most common question asked when meeting someone for the first time. Americans generally define themselves and others by profession.

Exercises

2: The majority of American politicians pay writers to write their speeches for them.
2: A congressman is a political representative who serves in the United States House of Representatives in Washington, D.C.
4: Exercise classes, along with health food and jogging, have become more and more popular for both men and women in the United States.

CHAPTER 3

Page 20: "Which One?"

Model

- "You should _____.", "Why don't you_____?", and "How about _____ing?" are common expressions for offering advice or suggestions.
- In line 4, "Hmm." indicates that the speaker is thinking and trying to remember.
- In line 5, Speaker A says "You remember." Speaker A is positive that Speaker B knows the object being talked about.

Page 21: "What's It Like There?"

Model

- With the expressions, "In my opinion . . . ," "If you ask me . . . ," and "As far as I'm concerned . . . ," a speaker focuses attention on the information to follow. These introductory phrases tell the listener that what follows is the speaker's opinion.
- When Americans plan a vacation, they are often primarily interested in knowing what the weather and the people are like.

Page 22: "As Far As I Know . . ."

Model

- "Do you/Would you by any chance know_____?" are polite ways of asking for information when approaching strangers.
- In line 3, Speaker B begins her answer to Speaker A's question by saying "As far as I know." This phrase is a common way to answer a question without appearing "too knowledgeable" and is therefore polite. Again in line 6, Speaker B is being polite when she says with uncertainty, "I don't think so." It isn't until Speaker A questions her certainty that Speaker B finally says "Yes, I'm positive."
- In line 4, "Hmm." indicates that Speaker A is thinking about or "digesting" this new information.
- This lesson illustrates the importance of the notion of time and schedule to Americans. In the model conversation, Speaker A is extremely concerned about the arrival time of the President. In the exercises, similar concern about time is expressed.

Page 23: "Did You Remember?"

Model

- "Uh-oh!" is a common expression used when someone suspects that something bad has happened.
- A family dog is considered important enough in the United States that if it is not fed on schedule, there is concern.
- In line 4, "Well," signals that the speaker has accepted the situation and is ready to decide on what action is to be taken.
- In line 4, "I guess one of us should go and do it." is similar to a suggestion. Speaker B is really suggesting that Speaker A do what was forgotten but does not directly say so.

Exercises

2: It is becoming more common in the United States for husbands and wives to share household chores such as cleaning, cooking, and setting the table.

Page 24: "Did You Hear?"

Model

- The announcement on the radio that schools are closed is probably due to a snowstorm. This is common during winter storms when traveling to school could be dangerous.

Exercises

4: City Hall is the location of the offices of city government.

Page 25: "Have You Heard the News?"

Model

- Declarative sentences spoken with question intonation are common ways of expressing surprise and disbelief. ("They're going to make the park across the street into a parking lot?!")

Model

- It is common and often considered polite to encourage a person telling a story by asking questions as the events unfold: "And then what did you do?", "What did you do after that?" This shows interest on the part of the listener.

CHAPTER 4

Page 32: "What Did You Say?"

Model

- In line 2, Speaker B says "I'm sorry." It is polite to apologize when asking for repetition. It is less polite simply to say "What?" or "Huh?"
- Playing "portable stereos" in public places is popular in the United States.

Page 33: "I'm Sorry. I Didn't Hear You"

Model

- By emphasizing the question word "WHEN . . . ?" or "WHAT . . . ?" Speaker B is indicating which piece of information he failed to hear or is not sure he heard correctly.

Pages 34–35: "Have You Got It?"

Model

- When asking strangers, the polite forms "Could you please tell me _____?, Could you possibly tell me_____?", and the like are more appropriate than direct questions such as "How do you get to the post office?"
- The expressions "(Have you) got it?, Do you follow me?, Okay?, Do you think you've got it now?" are used to check whether the person you are talking to has understood what you have said.
- The expressions "Let me see., Let me see if I understand., Let me see if I've got that (right)." are used to check your own understanding of what someone else has said. They would normally be followed by a repetition of the information that you are checking.
- The expressions "Uh-húh., Um-hḿm., Yes., (That's) right." are used to show that what the other speaker has said is correct. They give encouragement and tell the speaker to continue talking.
- In line 10, "Hmm . . ." indicates that the speaker has momentarily forgotten and is thinking.
- In line 13, by saying "Okay." the speaker indicates that she has understood.

Exercises

2: Self-service gas stations are popular in the United States. If gas customers pump their own gas, they usually pay less money for it.

Pages 36–37: "Are You With Me So Far?"

Model

- The expressions "Are you with me (so far)?, Okay (so far)?, Are you following me (so far)? Have you got all that?" are used to check another person's understanding of what you have said.
- The expressions "Yes, I'm with you., Now I've got it., I understand., I see., I'm with you." indicate that you have understood what the other person has said.

CHAPTER 5

Page 40: "Thanks For Saying So"

Model

- In line 2, Speaker B asks "Did you really like it?". This is a polite and gracious way to respond to a compliment. It indicates that the speaker is pleased, yet humble.
- Expressing gratitude is expected when responding to a compliment: "Thanks/Thank you (for saying so)., It's nice of you to say so/that."

Page 41: "You're Just Saying That!"

Model

- A typical way to make a compliment is by saying you like something and then telling why with a descriptive adjective. The superlative adjective is used to make a strong compliment.
- Instead of responding to a compliment with a simple "Thank you.", the following exchange is very common. The speaker responds to a compliment with an expression of disbelief: "Oh, go on! You're just saying that!" The speaker is not questioning the other person's sincerity, but instead is responding to the compliment with humility. The other person then normally insists that the compliment was sincere: "No, I mean it!, I'm (really) serious., I'm being honest with you."

3: "Interesting" is an adjective with little meaning. The speaker is either not sure how she feels about the painting, or, out of politeness, does not wish to say what she *really* thinks about it!

Page 42: "Just What I Had in Mind!"

Model

- A declarative sentence with question intonation is often used to check whether the other speaker is satisfied. For example, line 3: "It isn't too heavy?", line 7: "So you're satisfied with it?"

Page 43: "I'd Like a Refund, Please"

Model

- These expressions are used to find out the cause of a person's dissatisfaction: "What seems to be the problem (with it)?, What seems to be the matter (with it)?, What's the problem/the matter/wrong (with it)?"
- In the United States it is not unusual to return something you have purchased or you have received as a gift. Most department stores have a "Return Counter." A store will usually give a refund (return your money) and/or allow you to exchange the item for another and pay any difference in cost. Some stores won't give refunds or exchanges. If they don't, there are usually signs in the store telling a customer the store policy.
- In line 5, the customer uses the polite expression "I don't think so." or any of the alternatives rather than simply saying "No."
- In lines 9 and 11, the customer expresses surprise and disappointment when she exclaims "No refunds??" and "Oh."

Exercises

2: "Flashy"—very brightly colored, often with a wild pattern.

Page 44: "I Was a Little Disappointed"

Model

- By beginning a response with "To tell (you) the truth,/Honestly,/To be honest (with you)," the speaker is "setting the scene" for expressing a reaction of disappointment about something.
- "I was (a little) disappointed., I wasn't very pleased with it., It was a little disappointing." are expressions of disappointment and are also used as a way of complaining.

Page 45: "I'm Really Annoyed"

Model

- To be "mad at", "angry at", and "furious with" are very strong emotional states.
- Voicing a complaint to a friend is different from and much easier than complaining directly to the person responsible for the annoyance.
- In line 6, Speaker B says "I don't understand." Speaker B sees a direct and logical solution to the problem and cannot understand why Speaker A has not taken this step.
- The present continuous tense is often used to express a habitual action when emphasizing the frequency of the action.

Pages 46–47: "Would You Like to Get Together This Weekend?"

Model

- The questions "Would you like to_____?" and "Do you want to_____?" are very similar.
- By saying "Well," before answers and questions, the speakers are being polite by avoiding being too direct.
- In line 27, Speaker A says "But if you don't like seafood, we can go someplace else." He assumes that Speaker B will reject this suggestion since she has rejected every other one!
- After this long discussion, Speaker B says "Then it's settled." or any of the alternative lines. This indicates that a good decision for both speakers has been made.

CHAPTER 6

Page 50: "I'd Prefer a Baked Potato"

Model

- Restaurants in the United States almost always offer a choice of side dishes with the main course.
- When ordering items on a menu, the indefinite article "a/an" is normally used. For example, "I'll have a hamburger, a salad . . ." When the particular food being ordered is a specialty of the restaurant, the definite article is used. For example, "I'll have the chicken, the fish . . ." In this case, the particular dish is listed as a specialty on the menu and the definite article refers to that specific dish.
- The amount of cooking time for beef (steak, hamburger, roast beef) varies from "rare" (the shortest cooking time), "medium rare", "medium", "medium well" to "well done" (the longest cooking time).

Page 51: "I'd Much Rather See a Movie"

Model

- Accompanying a preference with expressions such as "To be honest" or "I think" and asking "Is that okay?" is a polite way of showing that the speaker is being considerate of the other person's feelings.

Pages 52–53: "A Serious Disagreement"

Model

- Line 1: "You've seemed troubled for the past few days." makes it clear that Speakers A and B are close enough friends so that A has noticed a change in B's behavior. Since they are good friends, Speaker A feels that it is appropriate to ask questions about B's problem.
- In line 3, "Well, to tell the truth" indicates that Speaker B is about to admit that there is a problem.
- In line 6, Speaker B says "To make a long story short, ..." This expression is used when people want to leave out details and get right to the main point.

Exercises

6: In the United States, older relatives are sometimes sent to special homes for senior citizens where they are taken care of by professionals.

7: A parish is a local church community.

9: In the United States, workers sometimes "go on strike" (stop working) if they have a serious disagreement with their employers.

Page 54: "It Doesn't Make Any Difference"

Model

- In line 2, "Oh." indicates that Speaker B is a little surprised; she probably hadn't been thinking about when the two were going to leave the party. The "I don't know." which follows further indicates that she doesn't have strong feelings about the matter.
- In line 4, Speaker A asks "You don't have any strong feelings about it?" Declarative sentences are often used as questions to check understanding.
- At large parties in the United States, guests do not necessarily arrive at the party or leave at specific times. Rather, they may arrive and leave as they wish.

Page 55: "It's Entirely Up to You"

Model

- In line 3, Speaker A is being very considerate and respectful of Speaker B by double-checking "Are you sure?" and by using the expression "I mean . . ." along with the polite statement which follows.
- In line 4, Speaker B is being equally as polite and considerate by saying "Honestly" along with his statements of indifference.

Exercises

5: "Security Blanket." Young children often choose a special blanket which they like to have with them at all times "for security." The child in Exercise 5 is about twelve years old and the mother feels that it is certainly time for her daughter to give up her "security blanket."

Pages 56–57: "The International Gourmet"

Model

- The expressions: "Well, . . . Let me see, . . . Let's see, . . . Hmm, . . . Okay, . . . Uh, . . . I think, . . . I guess . . ." are common ways of hesitating or "buying time" until you can think of what you want to say.

CHAPTER 7

Page 62: "I Promise"

Model

- To say the words "I promise" is to make a strong commitment to do something.
- In line 3, Speaker A emphasizes the importance of his request by double-checking with Speaker B: "You won't forget? It's really important."
- In line 4, recognizing how important this request is to Speaker A, Speaker B reassures him by saying "Don't worry. You can rely on me."

Exercises

5: In the United States, restaurant kitchens must maintain a standard of cleanliness determined by the local government in order to operate. A health inspector makes periodic visits to check that these standards are kept.

Page 63: "I Won't Let You Down"

Model

- In lines 3 and 5, Speaker A checks with Speaker B: "Can I depend on that?", "Now remember, I'm counting on you." The request is clearly important enough for the speaker to ask for reassurance twice.
- The single word expressions "Absolutely!, Definitely!, Positively!" indicate a strong statement of commitment.
- In line 5, Speaker A says "Okay." after Speaker B repeats his promise. This is a common way of responding to a promise and means "We both understand."
- A businessperson's workday normally begins at 9 a.m. and ends at 5 p.m. This businessman clearly needs his car by the end of the workday so that he can drive home.

Exercises

1: For a portion of the summer, children are often sent to overnight camp for fun and exercise (and as a vacation for their parents!).

Pages 64–65: "He Gave Me His Word"

Models

- "How come?" is equivalent to "Why?"
- In line 7, the expression "After all," implies "It's logical."

Exercises

4: "Overtime" means working more than the usual 40 hours per week.

Page 66: "I've Made a Decision"

Model

- The expression "You know" has a variety of meanings in English. In this instance, "You know" specifically introduces a new topic of conversation.
- "Gee!, Boy!, Wow!" are informal expressions for indicating surprise.
- In line 4, Speaker B expresses surprise and also comments on the importance of what Speaker A has announced: "That's a big decision!"

Page 67: "I'll Probably Stay Home and Read a Book"

Model

- The greeting "Hi! It's me!" is a very casual way to begin a telephone conversation. The speakers clearly know each other well enough to recognize one another's voice.
- In line 2, Speaker B answers "Oh, hi!" In this case, "Oh," indicates that Speaker B understands who "me" is in line 1.
- In line 3, Speaker A begins his question with "Tell me, . . ." This expression indicates that Speaker A wants to get directly to the point, the reason that he is calling.
- In line 3, when Speaker A asks "What are you doing this afternoon?", an invitation will probably follow. By responding "I'm not sure. I'll probably . . ." and asking "How about you?", Speaker B is communicating the fact that he is open to suggestions.
- In line 6, Speaker A says "Well," before announcing his plans. "Well," is used because the speaker wishes to avoid being too direct.

Page 68: "I Haven't Made Up My Mind Yet"

Model

- In line 1, "to ask" means "to invite."
- The subject "it" is sometimes dropped in casual conversation. In line 5, Speaker A says "Sounds like a difficult decision." ("[It] sounds like a difficult decision.")
- Similarly, short questions such as "Promise?" ("[Do you] promise?") and short answers such as "Promise." ("[I] promise.") are common in conversation.
- A prom is a formal dance, usually for high school students (ages 14–18). The "senior prom," a tradition in many U.S. high schools, is a dance attended by members of the senior class during the season of their graduation from high school.

Exercises

4: "Break up with"—end a romantic relationship with someone.

Page 69: "I Was Planning to Do Room 407 a Little Later"

Model

- In line 1, to "do" a room means to clean it.
- In line 2, Speaker B makes an excuse to a superior by stating a past intention ("I was planning to do it a little later.")

Pages 70–71: "I Changed My Mind"

Model

- In the United States, to say "Let's have lunch together sometime soon." is not necessarily an invitation. It is a common and polite way of saying good-bye.

CHAPTER 8

Page 74: "Do You Want Me to Wash the Dishes?"

Model

- "No. Don't worry about it." and "That's okay/all right." are polite ways of declining an offer.
- When making an offer and then being refused, Americans consider persuading or insisting to be polite and very appropriate.
- When responding to an offer, appreciation, in addition to gratitude, is the expected response.

Page 75: "Want Any Help?"

Model

- Making an observation ("I see you're changing the oil.") is a common way to initiate a conversation.
- Dropping the auxiliary and subject from the beginning of questions is common in casual conversation. For example, "(Do you) want any help?"
- "If you don't mind.", "If you wouldn't mind.", and "If it's no trouble." are common and polite ways of accepting an offer.

Pages 76–77: "Let Me Give You a Hand"

Model

- In line 6, Speaker A interrupts Speaker B as he is trying to refuse the offer. By doing this, along with strongly insisting and even ordering ("You're not moving that desk by yourself!"), Speaker A is not being rude. Rather, Speaker A is showing care and concern for Speaker B.

Page 78: "May I Help You?"

Model

- "May/Can I help you?" and "May/Can I assist you?" are common expressions used by salespeople when approaching customers.
- In line 2, Speaker B responds to Speaker A's offer of help by saying "I'm just looking." This expression is commonly used when you don't want a salesperson's assistance.
- In line 5, Speaker A begins to tell Speaker B that the store doesn't have any digital watches by saying "I'm afraid . . ." This expression is a polite way of giving bad news.
- In line 8, "I guess not." is a polite way of saying "No" to the salesperson.

Exercises

5: More and more "sugar free" food products are being produced in the United States, due to Americans' concern about their weight, the care of their teeth, and their general health.

Page 79: "Can I Do Anything to Help?"

Model

- In line 2, Speaker B hesitates when responding to Speaker A ("Well, uh . . .") because he has just been hurt and is not sure how to answer.
- Rollerskating on city streets is a popular activity in many parts of the United States.
- In line 5, Speaker A reacts to Speaker B's accident by saying "Oh, no!". By saying this he is indicating that he thinks the accident was a terrible thing and that he sympathizes with Speaker B.
- In most situations, asking for repetition by simply saying "Huh?" or "What?" is not polite. In this situation, however, Speaker B is somewhat confused and disoriented because of the accident.
- In line 9, Speaker A is offering his hand to help Speaker B up when he says "Well, here."
- When offering help, "Allow me . . ." is formal and very polite.

Exercises

1: To be "mugged" means to be attacked by a thief on the street.

Page 80: "I'm Very Grateful to You"

Model

- In this conversation, Speaker A strongly insists on thanking Speaker B because the favor (lending the calculator) was an important one.

Exercises

5: "Fix someone up"—arrange for two people to meet each other with the hope that they will become romantically involved.

Page 81: "Words Can't Express . . ."

Model

- At a formal award ceremony such as this, very formal and flowery language is appropriate and expected.

CHAPTER 9

Pages 84–85: "Is Smoking Allowed Here?"

Models

- The passive construction and the pronouns "they" and "you" are often used when referring to some authority. The identity or source of this authority is not known or not important.
- In models 2 and 4, Speaker A says "Oh, okay." as a way of accepting the negative response he has just been given by Speaker B.

Page 86: "Please Don't Pick the Flowers"

Model

- In line 1, Speaker A is trying to be polite and not seem critical of Speaker B's actions by using the less direct "Excuse me, but I don't think . . . ."
- In line 5, "Hmm." indicates that Speaker B is considering this new information while reading the sign.

Page 87: "Can I Possibly Have the Car Tonight?"

Model

- In line 1, before Speaker A directly asks for permission, he says "Could I ask you a favor?" He does this to signal to Speaker B that he wishes to make a request.
- Saying "Yes" tentatively can be done by using the expressions "I guess so.", "I suppose so.", and "I don't see (any reason) why not."
- In lines 6–7, ". . . it wouldn't hurt to ask." is a non-direct way of telling Speaker A that he should ask his mother.

Exercises

5: A hot tub (pronounced "HOT tub") is a large tub filled with very warm water in which one or more people sit to relax. Hot tubs are very popular in the United States, especially on the West Coast.

Pages 88–89: "Would You Mind If I Served Leftovers for Dinner?"

Models

- "Leftovers" consist of food not eaten at a previous meal that is for use in a later meal.
- In line 3 of the first model, "No," indicates a positive response to Speaker A's request for permission.

Exercises

2: To "skip" dessert means to go without it.
8: A "teddy bear" is a stuffed toy in the shape of a bear that is named after Theodore "Teddy" Roosevelt, the twenty-sixth president of the United States.

Page 90: "I'd Rather You Didn't"

Model

- The expressions "You see, . . ." "The reason is . . ." are used to preface an admission.
- In line 3, "Oh," indicates that Speaker A was expecting a positive response to his request. He acknowledges the negative response when he says "okay."
- In line 5, "Oh," indicates that Speaker A understands Speaker B's reason for denying permission. Speaker A also politely apologizes for not knowing the reason beforehand.

Page 91: "I Can't Do That Without an Authorization"

Model

- In line 2, Speaker B politely begins his negative response by saying "I'm afraid I can't. . . ."
- In line 4, "Oh?" indicates that Speaker A is surprised and a little disappointed at the negative response.
- In line 5, Speaker B begins his explanation by saying "Well,". Here "Well," signals the beginning of a long, yet definitive explanation.
- In this conversation, Speaker B apologizes for not having the authority himself to do what Speaker A wants. Speaker A's "I understand." indicates that she recognizes that another authority is responsible and not Speaker B.

INDEX OF FUNCTIONS AND CONVERSATION STRATEGIES